ON ACQUIRING WISDOM

A NON-EMBODIED SPIRITUAL PERSPECTIVE
CHANNELLED BY PETER CALVERT & KEITH HILL

PETER CALVERT & KEITH HILL
Learning Who You Are
The Matapaua Conversations
The Kosmic Web

PETER CALVERT
Guided Healing
Agapé and the Hierarchy of Love

KEITH HILL
Experimental Spirituality
Practical Spirituality
Psychological Spirituality
What Is Really Going On?
Where Do I Go When I Meditate?
How Did I End Up Here?

RELATED BOOKS

PETER CALVERT, RICHARD BENTLEY
CAROLYN LONGDEN, TRISHA WREN
People of the Earth

KEITH HILL
The New Mysticism

ON ACQUIRING WISDOM

A Reincarnational Perspective

Peter Calvert & Keith Hill

First edition published in 2024 by Attar Books
Auckland, New Zealand.

Copyright © Peter Calvert & Keith Hill 2024

The right of Peter Calvert and Keith Hill to be identified as the joint authors of this work is asserted according to Section 96 of the Copyright Act 1996.

Paperback ISBN 978-1-0670142-3-0
Casebook ISBN 978-1-0670142-4-7

All rights reserved. Copying and distributing passages excerpted from this book for the purpose of sharing and discussing is permitted on the condition that the source of each excerpt is fully acknowledged, and such excerpts are not onsold. Otherwise, except for fair dealing or brief passages quoted in a newspaper, magazine, radio, television or internet review, no part of this book may be reproduced in any form or by any means, or in any form of binding or cover other than that in which it is published, without permission in writing from the Publisher. This same condition is imposed on any subsequent purchaser.

Cover photograph by Keith Hill

Attar Books is a New Zealand publisher which focuses on work that explores today's spiritual experiences, culture, concepts and practices. For more information visit our website:

Attar Books
www.attarbooks.com

Contents

	Preface	7

ON ACQUIRING WISDOM

	Introduction	11
1	**Defining the Context**	
	The need for fresh wisdom	23
	The process of acquiring wisdom	24
	Features of this teaching	27
	Wisdom is perennially present	30
2	**The Field of First Cause**	
	The dynamic of emergent identity	33
	Freedom and consequence	36
3	**Modelling a Multi-Life Journey**	
	Delineating spiritual space	40
	Locating identity in spiritual space	41
	Making choices produces location change	44
4	**Balance and Serenity**	
	The depth of serenity	47
	An impediment to serenity	50
5	**Ecstasy, Intimacy and Death**	
	Additional parameters of love	53
	Intimacy and giving out love	54
	Moving on after death	56
	A recitation for the dying	57

6	**Negative After-Life Possibilities**	
	After-death mobility	59
	Those who do not move on easily	61
	Mara and others	62
	Spiritual retribution	63
7	**The Complications of Dispersal**	
	On the memory of being spirit	65
	Avoiding enthusiastic conversion	67
8	**This Perspective is Not Moralistic**	
	Redefining self-aggrandisement	69
	Judging choices wrong is wrong	70
	On validly making choices	72
9	**Haric Level Perceptions**	
	A less benevolent identity	74
	Historical observations	75
	An authoritative caduceus interpretation	78
10	**Concluding Remarks**	80
	Appendices	
1	Definitions and co-ordinate descriptions	85
2	*The Transmission of Wisdom* by Roger Walsh	87
3	The Universe is in a multiverse	91
4	A confused climber	98
5	A mischievous spirit	102
6	The plane of morality	108
	To the reader	110

Preface

Peter Calvert and I first met in 2008, at a book fair in Tauranga, New Zealand, where Peter was presenting his first channelled work, *Agapé and the Hierarchy of Love*. I bought a copy, started reading, and was immediately drawn in. The material offered a rational, scientifically-oriented approach to spiritual development that made a lot of sense. But as much as the text, I was drawn to the standpoint from which it was written. The identities Peter was channelling were looking down on human existence from *way* above. They were knowledgeable without being dogmatic, exact without being stuffy, and they had a sense of humour. What especially attracted me was that they offered a very relevant contemporary take on metaphysical and spiritual matters.

As a result, I offered to help Peter edit his next channelled book, *Guided Healing*. While working on it I decided meeting Peter presented a unique opportunity to ask a group of non-embodied identities, if that's who he was communicating with, some serious questions. I consequently put together a list of what became one hundred questions on "big" topics, such as the creation of the universe, how the spiritual and physical connect, and the purpose of life on Earth. The answers Peter received surprised us both. They went far beyond what either of us had anticipated, and opened up an entirely new—at least, for us—way of conceiving reality.

The answers Peter received, and the diary he kept while working on them, I edited into our first collaborative book, *The Matapaua Conversations*. Since then our collaboration has blossomed, resulting in eleven books to date, channelled by one or both of us. Beyond this, during the past three decades Peter has channelled well over a million words (and counting), which he has archived.

On Acquiring Wisdom is a continuation of this work. It examines an ancient concept from a contemporary perspective. We view this book as sitting between, and to some extent overlapping with, two previous books, *Learning Who You Are* and *The Kosmic Web*. The first is an entry-level text that introduces the viewpoint, ideas and key terminology used by the non-embodied identities we are communicating with, while the second details their cosmological, biological, cultural and metaphysical thinking.

What differentiates this material from traditional teachings is that its conceptual frame is non-religious, preferring to link spiritual processes to current scientific and cultural knowledge and language. It explores the spiritual aspects of our existence in ways that sync with how we see the world in the twenty-first century.

Keith Hill, editor

ON ACQUIRING WISDOM

Introduction

The goal of acquiring wisdom has a substantial history. Solomon, king of Israel during the tenth century BCE, has long been revered by followers of Judaism, Christianity and Islam as one the greatest of the wise. The depth of his insight was famously revealed in a story that two arguing women came to him, each claiming a baby as theirs. To resolve the situation, Solomon proposed he cut the baby in half and give each an equal portion. One woman instantly declared the other could have her baby. Thus Solomon identified the real mother.

Solomon's wisdom became proverbial, resulting in a book, *The Wisdom of Solomon*—written long after he lived, by others in his name—and to a new genre of writing, Jewish wisdom literature, which delved into the moral and spiritual complications of human interactions.

However, Solomon offers just one model of those who possess wisdom. He was wise in the ways of the world. Others were wise in the ways of the soul. They include mystics such as Lao Tzu, Siddhartha Gautama and Zarathustra, the founders of Taoism, Buddhism and Zoroastrianism, who offered original insights into the nature of metaphysical reality, that is, of what exists beyond, within and in parallel to the physical. Innumerable mystics through the ages, practitioners in these and other traditions, have similarly been acclaimed as wise due to the depth of their spiritual insights.

Proverbs, another book ascribed to Solomon but compiled from several unnamed writers' thoughts on wisdom, begins with the statement that its teaching provides "instruction in prudent behaviour, doing what is right and just and fair; giving prudence to the simple, [and] knowledge and discretion to the young." (1: 2-4) This instruction is moral. It emphasises the need to obey God, whose guidance is encoded in religious laws, do good to others in order to gain the reward of God's approval, and to avoid those who would lead one into evil. This is a religious view of wisdom.

However, one section in *Proverbs* offers a very different, much more abstract, concept. Here wisdom is depicted as being formed "at the very beginning, when the world came to be." (8:23). Wisdom is described as having accompanied Yahweh when he laid the heavens, established a boundary for the seas, and set the foundations of the Earth. This is a metaphysical concept of wisdom as a divine quality that pre-existed the creation of the world and humanity's coming into being.

Thus we have two concepts of wisdom. The first is moral, wisdom being possessed by those who wisely navigate their way through our complex, testing world. The second is metaphysical, that wisdom exists far beyond us, in a meta-reality that transcends human life. In *Proverbs*, wisdom as a moral quantity present in social interactions is described in detail, but its existence on the metaphysical level is expounded only sketchily.

However, millennia earlier Mesopotamian and Egyptian cultures had described transcendent wisdom in more rigour. Enki, the Sumerian god of knowledge, water and craft, is considered to have drawn on his wisdom to create and order the heavens and Earth. This is essentially the same idea as is presented in *Proverbs*, although in the Judaic text wisdom is depicted as passively observing God as he created the world, whereas Enki actively used his wisdom to create and order it.

For the Egyptians, several gods embodied aspects of wisdom. Saa was considered to possess deep insight into the nature of the world, but kept his wisdom to himself. Thoth was the god who brought wisdom to humanity in the forms of hieroglyphs, science, art, magic and sound judgement. Thoth was married to Maat, who symbolised order—as with Enki, wisdom and order are linked—while their daughter, Seeshat, invented writing and thus gave human beings the ability to record the knowledge and wisdom they acquired. Here wisdom is conceived as an intermediary between the meta-realm of the gods and the physical realm of humanity. It is characterised as having divine, godly qualities—orderliness, sagacity, insight—but manifests in specific human skills: writing, art, science, magic, sound judgement. The Egyptians thus viewed wisdom as simultaneously divine and human.

The limitation of the Sumerian and Egyptian concepts of wisdom is that they are presented in mythological form, as anthropomorphic gods. For us today, Saa, Thoth, Seeshat and the others are not gods; they are personifications of abstract concepts. They are characters in stories invented to explain what happens in a mysterious world.

By 600 BCE the Greeks began separating those abstract concepts from their mythological wrappings. To this process Pythagoras, the most influential of the early Greek thinkers, gave the name *philosophy*, a composite of two Greek words, *philo* (love) and *sophia* (wisdom). Philosophy, then, is the love of wisdom. It is worth briefly considering Pythagorean philosophy here, as its approach to wisdom is reflected in what follows.

Philosophy for Pythagoras and his followers[1] was a spiritual practice, which combined self-transformational exercises such as meditation, fasting and ritual worship with intellectual enquiry. Intellectual enquiry, in the way Pythagoras applied it, signalled an important break with the past. For Pythagoras, the world was not created by gods like Enki, Saa or Yahweh, nor was it the result of abstract principles such as wisdom, order or sound judgement imagined as anthropomorphic gods. Instead, the world was ordered by number.

Aristotle records in his *Metaphysics* that the origin of this conceptual breakthrough was via music. Pythagoras discerned a numerical relationship between the lengths of strings on a lyre and the notes they produced, and that musical harmony results from the strings being organised in strict ratios: 2:1, 3:2, 4:3. He may have gleaned this knowledge from the Babylonians, because he travelled widely as a young man, through Egypt, Israel, Mesopotamia, and possibly as far as India, synthesising the knowledge he found. However, his next step seems to have been his original idea. Pythagoras extended the notion of musical harmony derived from ratios to the world, applying it to the cosmos—planets wheeling

---

[1] For a scholarly but very readable summary of what we know of Pythagoras's life and ideas see *Pythagoras and the Pythagoreans* (2001) by Charles H. Khan.

through the heavens—and to the earth-bound—dividing physical forms into basic geometric shapes. Astronomy, geometry, arithmetic and music were subsequently valued by Greek thinkers as sister studies, united in number.

Pythagorean cosmological harmony subsequently gave rise to the concept of the music of the spheres, which two millennia later influenced Johannes Kepler when he conceived the laws of orbital motion. The idea that number is fundamental to all physical phenomena also provided the foundation on which Isaac Newton constructed his physical laws of motion and light.

But Pythagoras had another set of ideas as innovative as thinking number underpins the world. This is that the human psyche (soul) survives the body's death and subsequently reincarnates. He was reputed to remember several of his own past lives, and to be able to perceive aspects of others' past lives. Reincarnation became the second major strand of his philosophy. He subsequently established a school in southern Italy, where his students lived communally and everyone was united in the goal of purifying their psyches, living a knowing life, and preparing themselves for the afterlife.

Those joining the community undertook a five-year probationary period. Only after completing this were they allowed into the inner sanctum where Pythagoras' doctrines were directly shared. Teaching occurred orally; nothing was written down. This was standard Greek practice at the time, spoken words being viewed as alive, whereas written words were considered to have lost their animation. By the time of Plato, who wrote his philosophic dialogues 150 years later, the taboo against writing had largely lost its cultural grip. Nonetheless, even for Plato certain ideas were considered too significant to write down. These ideas, called "unwritten doctrines", were only shared orally with senior students.

In addition to the taboo against writing, no Pythagorean was permitted to share what they learned with outsiders. This was also in keeping with Greek norms: the annual Eleusinian mysteries required initiates to vow never to publicly discuss what they experienced. This prohibition was so universally respected that despite the mysteries being held over a period of 2,000 years, we have no record of what occurred at their climax, nor what revelation lay at heart of the mysteries.

Unfortunately for Pythagoras's community, not telling outsiders what they were doing led the sceptical to imagine the worst. Some of the Pythagoras's peers considered him a charlatan and his wisdom fraudulent, while those living near the community became so suspicious of what they were *really* up to that they eventually broke in, killed many, and burned their buildings to the ground. It's possible Pythagoras died at this time. He was aged in his early 70s.

Pythagoras and his community may have ended then, but his philosophy continued to have a powerful social and intellectual impact. The survivors broke into two groups: the *akousmatikoi*, who continued to live according to religious and purification rituals embodied in Pythoragas' sayings, and the *mathēmatikoi*, who emphasised the number aspects of his teaching. Both groups had an influence on their fellow Greeks. Pythagoreans were revered as healers and interpreters of dreams, and their sound moral judgements were employed to create laws governing cities. Others became leading mathematicians and engineers. Philolaus, a mathematician born two decades after Pythagoras died, wrote the first book detailing Pythagorean cosmology, in which he proposed the Earth was not the centre of the cosmos—geocentrism otherwise prevailed throughout Europe until the 1600s. Archytas, a friend of Plato, was a mathematician, politician and general who devised weapons for his city's defence, as well as to attack their enemy. He wrote several books detailing Pythagorean philosophy. Unfortunately, none survive.

Plato is the writer who preserved much of what we know of Pythagoras's philosophy. After his teacher Socrates died he sought out prominent Pythagoreans, learning from them and incorporating their teaching in his thought. While aspects of Pythagorean philosophy are scattered throughout Plato's dialogues, two stand out for the fullness of their exposition.

In *Phaedrus* Plato presents the Pythagorean view that the soul is immortal but needs to purify itself to access wisdom. Plato elaborates this doctrine into an allegorical narrative, suggesting that during a soul's life in a body it rides a chariot pulled by two horses, one white and one black. The white horse is beautiful and good and strives to pull the soul up, into the pure intellectual and spiritual realm, while the black horse wants to pull the soul down, into an impure, self-destructive, sense-dominated life.

In order to fly high into the heavens the soul needs to adopt philosophy and its purification practices. Once sufficiently wise it no longer reincarnates.

In *Timaeus*, Plato elaborates on Pythagorean cosmological ideas. Philolaus wrote that everything in the cosmos[2] is a harmony of two forces: the Unlimited, from which everything in the cosmos originates, and the Limited, a range of principles that shape, and therefore limit, everything existing in the world. Through his narrator, Timaeus, Plato seeks to explain how what exists potentially in the Unlimited forms the limited natural world. Generating his own mythology, he proposes that a divine craftsman, which he calls the demiurge, created the physical world by drawing from and recreating, imperfectly and in lesser form, what pre-exists in the perfect, transcendent realm. Numbers and geometry play a key role in this process, giving the demiurge the means to create the world, to set the Earth, Sun, planets and Moon in motion and in their correct places, to create human beings, and to account for the reincarnation of their souls. (Timaeus also takes time out to discuss the history of Atlantis, the story of which, Plato explains, was preserved by Egyptian priests.)

The philosophies of Pythagoras and Plato were revived in late antiquity, from the second century BCE to the fourth century CE, influencing numerous philosophical and mystical schools, including those of Hermeticism, Judaism, Gnosticism and, later, Sufism and Kabbalah. These schools kept alive the love of wisdom that beat at the heart of ancient Greek philosophy so that it survived well into the seventeenth century.

On the other hand, and despite their emphasis on number and rational analysis, Pythagoras and Plato included gods and the divine in their philosophies, which reduces their relevance today. In addition, many of their claims about the nature of reality were entirely speculative and have been shown not to be true. More problematically, today's scientific and academic thought rejects the idea that any kind of meta-reality exists beyond the physical. The world is considered to be wholly, and only, material. This is in spite of Pythagorean number laying the foundations for our mathematically-based sciences, and the word *academic* being derived from the Academy, the school Plato established to pursue philosophic enquiry.

---

[2] The English word cosmos comes from the Greek, *kosmos*, meaning order.

Today philosophy has radically diverged from its beginnings. It is largely sceptical in outlook, and functions in tandem with scientific materialism. That is, it assumes reality is limited to the physical, that the metaphysical of any kind doesn't exist, and that wisdom is irrelevant.

Our modern outlook has pluses. Specialisations developed over the last four hundred years, when the scientific observational method began being applied at scale, have enabled us to acquire insights into the nature of the world that would astonish our philosopher forebears. Yet while we know a great deal more than they did about the natural forces that power the world, we cannot claim to be wiser than them. We know more about the *how* of the world—how it functions physically, how to extract minerals from it, how to transform them into commodities—but we are far from being, like Solomon, wise in the *ways* of the world. Socially and culturally, unruly, ugly, destructive forces dominate our lives. As a species, we are struggling to cope with the numerous "genies" our knowledge has let out of their bottles. If humanity ever needed wisdom, now is the time.

That conclusion leads us to this book, which reconsiders the concept of wisdom on its meta, social and psychospiritual levels, and offers a view regarding how wisdom remains relevant to us today. Clearly, collectively, we need to acquire wisdom. But to do so we also need a fresh perspective on wisdom, one relevant to our twenty-first century perspective.

The impetus to seek a fresh understanding of wisdom, as offered here, initially came from Peter, after he had discovered an essay published in the *Journal of Transpersonal Research* and written by Roger Walsh, a professor of psychiatry, philosophy and anthropology. Peter observes: "When I first accessed the paper by Walsh ten years ago, I felt a thrill of recognition that it captured the essence of my endeavours in life. Of course, I had no idea how long it might be before I could directly access the classes of knowledge he identified. Yet it set a context for a worthwhile goal and direction for my personal yearning."

Walsh's paper, *The Transmission of Wisdom: The Task of Gnostic Intermediaries*,[3] begins with the following summary:

---

[3] The essay is reprinted in full in Appendix 2.

> Wisdom is one of the seven qualities that authentic contemplative traditions aim to foster. This wisdom is said to be a combination of existential understanding and practical life skills, as well as transrational, intuitive insight.

Walsh is acknowledging the same dual thrust of wisdom recognised in ancient times: understanding complex human situations and having the life skills to negotiate through them, and deep intuitive insight into the broader and more expansive meta-reality in which we exist. Using Greek terminology, Walsh names these two facets *sophia* and *phronesis*, the first being deep understanding, the second practical life skills. The two lay the foundations for wisdom. Despite his emphasis on half of wisdom involving its practical application, Walsh sees wisdom as most commonly acquired by contemplatives, those who, like the ancient Pythagoreans, devote their lives to inward practices. This leads him to expand his definition:

> Contemplative wisdom finds its deepest basis in a direct, intuitive transcendental apprehension. This wisdom has many names, such as *gnosis*[4] (Christianity), *jnana* (Hinduism), *prajna* (Buddhism), *hokhmah* (Judaism), and *ma'rifah* (Islam). This transrational wisdom, which we might call *transnoia*,[5] seems to foster *sophia* and *phronesis*, while also adding further depth and richness to them. It is therefore not surprising that some of history's greatest contemplatives have also been regarded as being among history's wisest sages, e.g. Christianity's Dionysus, Hinduism's Shankara, Islam's Ibn Arabi, Kashmir Shaivism's Abinavagupta, Neo-Confucianism's Wang Yang-ming, and the Buddha.

Identifying individuals from specific traditions brings us to the issue of the wise sharing what they learn. Walsh calls these individuals gnostic intermediaries, their function being to transmit what they have acquired to

---

[4] *Gnosis*, Greek for knowledge, used to denote experiential spiritual knowledge.
[5] *Trans*, Latin for across or beyond, *noia*, Greek for thought.

others who wish to learn what they know. Walsh proposes the transmission of wisdom by gnostic intermediaries requires three things.

> First, it requires cultivating wisdom through contemplative practices; second, mastering the linguistic and conceptual system of the community to whom you wish to communicate; and third, translating aspects of wisdom into this linguistic and conceptual system.
> This is obviously a demanding task. However, it is also an essential one for our time, as scholars and practitioners seek to understand the deeper significance of contemplative practices, psychologies, and philosophies.

Walsh's first point is self-evident. His second underscores the issue that those who wish to communicate complex concepts need to be versed in the key ideas of their time. They also need to have a command of a suitable vocabulary to communicate those ideas. This leads to Walsh's third point, that they need to be able to translate one set of insights, and their facilitating practices, into culturally relevant concepts and language. This last is a creative task, not just one of information sharing.

Translation is difficult. It is made more difficult because in the past, while many contemplatives sought to share their insights, they often faced extreme pushback from religious authorities, who preferred intellectual conformity to consensually agreed doctrines and were opposed to "direct, intuitive transcendental apprehension". Randomly selected examples of conservative pushback include the treatment of St John of the Cross, who was imprisoned and beaten by his fellow monks; the great late medieval Christian mystic, Meister Eckhart, who was accused of blasphemy; the Zen master, Hui Neng, who after receiving the symbols of transmission from his teacher was instructed to leave so his disgruntled fellow monks would not be able to kill him; and the Gnostic Cathars of France, Spain and Italy, who were hunted, tortured and exterminated by the Inquisition on behalf of the Catholic Church.

Nonetheless, what aided the efforts of "gnostic intermediaries" to communicate what they learned is that they and their conservative opponents were all embedded in the same social and intellectual milieu. They were all brought up sharing the same texts, rituals, doctrines and basic religious outlook. This made it easier for those gnostic intermediaries to share their innovative doctrines: everyone shared the same myths and doctrines. Conversely, that was what made them dangerous to religious authorities, who feared they would lead too many away from the common ground.

Today we have two great hindrances to the sharing of wisdom. First, the religious modes of mystical expression used for over three millennia are no longer considered of value by the religious. They have little to no place for mystical experiencing, and so ignore genuine metaphysical enquiry. Second, the tenets of scientific naturalism dominate today's public thinking and attitudes, and they similarly reject metaphysical enquiry. Neither conservative religionists nor scientific naturalists have any interest in the self-developmental practices promoted by ancient philosophers, nor in their spiritual goal of acquiring wisdom.

Yet, as Walsh proposes, having contemplatives share what they have discovered remains essential for our time. Their insights continue to have intrinsic value.

That brings us to the methodology that has produced this book. The following text was channelled by Peter during a two week retreat he undertook in 2021, in a small town situated at the bottom of New Zealand's South Island. His motivation was to receive a response from our non-embodied mentors to Walsh's thoughts on wisdom.

Our mentors are non-embodied entities constituted of between 800 and 1,200 individuals who have completed their cycles of reincarnations on this planet. Each having lived an embodied existence an average of one thousand times, they may be considered to be wise in both the ways of the human world and in the ways that human consciousness exists in the spiritual realm. As such, this text is a step on from the ancient Greek philosophers' thoughts on reincarnation, given our forebears had to speculate to a degree, whereas the mentors offer their observations as a result of direct personal perception and experience.

This book follows multiple texts Peter has previously channelled. Those texts include over 3010 meditation sessions, which has resulted in the production of an expansive body of archived channelled communications, and a number of books produced jointly with Keith (see attarbooks.com). Given this background, Peter and Keith have considerable experience in performing the role of what Walsh calls gnostic intermediary. Regarding this, Peter observes:

"We have done our personal best to cultivate wisdom via contemplative practice, which is ongoing. We have attempted to master the linguistic and conceptual systems of our culture and respective fields of study. And we have each translated such wisdom as has come to us, through generating in some cases novel metaphors, but mostly by adapting the language of our culture to this task."

Significantly, he adds, "Being new, the material of this book cannot claim to be a tradition." The old wisdom traditions have lost momentum. And, as yet, we have no widely adopted new traditions to replace them. Clearly, innumerable seekers wishing to explore their meta-reality are still attracted to the old spiritual, philosophic and mystical traditions—because they remain the best and most widely known sources of philosophic wisdom, and as such still have inherent value.

Yet, at the same time, today numerous explorers and thinkers are seeking to discover wisdom just as our ancient forebears did, but in ways best suited to their interests and abilities. Their explorations are multi-faceted, multi-cultural, multi-contextual and trans-national. Much that is new, or that reformulates the old in new ways, is being presented across the world, by people working in different languages and using diverse conceptual frameworks.

This book contributes to that effort. It is also part of the work Peter and Keith have carried out for eight decades, separately and together, to contribute to this opening out of understanding, to this re-orientation of the foundational thinking regarding wisdom. Of our need for wisdom the mentors state:

> Wisdom is grounded in awareness of ultimate things. As people become immersed in the details of their lives, seeking what they desire and are able to gather in the time allotted them, they lose sight of ultimate things—including the need to develop

their personal psychospiritual nature, and the need to be aware of the social and cultural momentums in which they live, which both aid and hinder their development. A commonly shared belief is that ultimate things are unimportant, because they are so remote. This is a mistake. Ultimate things form a comprehensive, and comprehensible, background to every action, every awareness, every time-bound event. Ultimate things underpin every life, human or otherwise.

Hence all cultures, however unconscious they may be that they are doing so, provide a few individuals sufficient time and freedom to escape the ordinary responsibilities necessary to their physical survival, and give them the opportunity to contemplate ultimate things. This individual [Peter] is one of an extended number of similarly focused individuals.

To repeat: What follows is a text channelled by Peter and edited by Keith.[6] Its aim is to present a non-embodied view of wisdom, consider what facets of human existence wisdom applies to, and how it may be acquired.

Following the same emphasis adopted by Pythagoras over two millennia ago, it explores the need to undertake a self-developmental practice in order to prepare oneself to acquire knowledge of "ultimate things", to use the intellect to rationally dissect what is discovered—and, at times, to use number to do so—and to apply what is extracted from experience to having a fulfilling lifetime, fulfilling both for oneself and providing fulfillment to others, on whatever level that might be.

Behind it all is the assumption that human existence is reincarnational in nature, that developing *sophia* and *phronesis* is a multi-life task, and that development occurs as a result of repeatedly living, attempting, making mistakes, learning, reliving, relearning, perfecting, then attempting new tasks, developing new skills, making new mistakes, achieving new insights, over and over, until one achieves what could be said to be the ultimate goal of the entire process of human incarnation: becoming wise.

---

[6] This Introduction and footnotes are by Keith.

CHAPTER 1

Defining the Context

The need for fresh wisdom

Wisdom is an ancient concept. Historically, wisdom has involved collecting information, then collating it to construct an ordered doctrine, often presented in written form, that may be used by others to confront and make sense of the complexities of their existence. But doing so has had its limitations.

Over the millennia few have acknowledged the extent of human ignorance. In particular, humanity's propensity to project anthropomorphic assumptions onto what is unknown—including imagining parental substitutes living in the sky or underworld—has resulted in the creation of what may be termed "worst-case scenarios". These include that gods or a God punish human beings for their transgressions via natural disasters, that people are born good or evil, and that if believers don't do what their betters tell them they will be eternally punished. These "worst-case scenarios"—which, we note, are entirely human inventions—have been shared for thousands of years both orally, through religious proselytising, and archived in numerous texts.

In this context, we are introducing what may be termed a "best case scenario". By doing so, we are deliberately interrupting the course of human existence. Why? Because it is time to correct misapprehensions. We make no claim to be offering Truth, with a capital T. Rather, we are merely stating what follows because it is accurate. After reading it others may not think so. We have no difficulty with that. Nonetheless, the task we have undertaken here is to present an *accurate* description of what wisdom encompasses.

Looking back at past formulations of wisdom, readers will appreciate that their forebears lacked today's analytical tools. This lack led them to interpret a broad sweep of human phenomena and behaviour in unwise, and frequently quite ignorant, ways. That is to be expected, because their analysis originated in limited attitudes that rose in the very beginnings of the human experiment.[1] Those beginnings now being far in the past, it is appropriate to abandon ancient formulations as a reference point, and instead consider wisdom in humanity's present context.

This context assumes that humanity is universally educated, that those who wish it may become universally well informed, and that everyone may exchange information across the globe, via universally accessible communication systems. This is a very different situation to humanity's earliest beginnings, when, metaphorically speaking, humans first stood upright, looked into the heavens, and considered their place in the world.

Yet the information now in circulation is too much to be processed by any single mind, or even by any single group. Given this, we acknowledge we need to be careful in how we introduce and organise the ideas we intend to discuss. To ensure what we wish to share is relevant to a broad band of enquiring people, we also need to generalise, which means discussing wisdom within the largest possible set of principles.

The process of acquiring wisdom

Those involved in current industrial processes for organising information have invented the developmental platform.[2] We will make use of the concept of developmental platform, and its related terminology, to begin this discussion of wisdom.

---

[1] The idea that all life on this planet is an experiment is elaborated in several books. *Learning Who You Are* is a useful introduction to the concept, *The Kosmic Web* sets the topic into a wider cosmological, biological and metaphysical context, and *Experimental Spirituality* considers experimentation in relation to personal life-by-life psychospiritual development.

In the context of acquiring wisdom, the developmental platform is human embodiment. Embodiment provides the fundamental architecture on which human experience is built.

Human experience itself may be characterised as a process of information gathering. The experience of being embodied provides access to myriad variables. These are largely organised around relationships with other people. They include the situations, creatures and objects that are part of those relationships, and individual preferences in relation to them. The knowledge each accrues enables them to distinguish between what is optimal and suboptimal for them personally, information they subsequently use to select their next sets of relationships in subsequent lives.

The density of information extracted from the experience of "ephemeral being", that is, of the physically embodied person, far outweighs what can be obtained in the realm of non-embodied being. We use the term "ephemeral being" to express the paradoxical relationship between time and being. Time is ephemeral. The term "ephemeral being" refers to a living physical body and its emergent identity and personality, which exist only for that body's lifetime, and so are ephemeral. The being that acquires the information accrued by its ephemeral embodied identity is not embedded in time, and therefore is not ephemeral.

We associate the idea of a developmental platform with embodiment. Embodiment provides the basic platform, which an individual existing in the realm of spiritual being uses to construct a series of ephemeral identities, each of which facilitates the acquisition of diverse forms of information. An individual's overarching aim during serial embodiment is to progressively minimise suboptimal personal characteristics, opportunities and experiences, and to engineer increasingly optimal characteristics, opportunities and experiences.

We use this metaphor to distance embodiment and what it involves

---

[2] In the computer industry, the term "developmental platform" refers to a foundational level of computer coding, which developers build on to create more complex applications. An example is Flutter, released by Google, which provides a standard base code that developers use to build a wide range of mobile, web and desktop computer applications. Simply, a developmental platform provides a set of standards that underpin diverse applications.

from traditional opinions and attitudes. In particular, we wish to widen the frame of reference, focusing not on the details of identity and its personality development—which are assumed to be a product of the local mind—and proposing instead that identity exists to gather information.

In this way, identity may be viewed as a process related to industrial product development, the ultimate product being an experienced, knowledgeable and loving identity on the spiritual level. To achieve this, a spiritual being uses an extended series of ephemeral identities, each successively built on the same basic architecture provided by embodiment.

To reinforce this line of thinking, we offer another platform metaphor. An electric vehicle, comprising motive power, power source, chassis and attached wheels, is a transportation mechanism designed to provide mobility. But this is merely a basic platform, to which a wide range of enhancements are added. These include additions for styling and performance, which are made to appeal to buyers' personal tastes, as well as to the practical issue of how many people the vehicle is to transport. The variety of electric cars, utility vehicles, vans, trucks, buses, trains, etc, attest to the diversity of possibilities. A significant range of enhancements are added to the simple electric transportation platform.

This provides an analogous situation to that of extra-physical identity using the human body as a developmental platform, to which it adds enhancements, life after life, in order to develop its permanent identity.

A radical rearrangement of perspective

We offer these examples to decouple the discussion from the idealisations, concept sets and terminologies that have been developed over the millennia. Thus, to clarify the process of how identity develops, we offer a rearrangement of longstanding perspectives. In fact, a radical rearrangement.

It is radical because attachment to a particular body is not required. Attachment to a particular culture or a particular set of beliefs is not required. Instead, one needs to be willing to consider the process of identity development from a vantage point independent of personality, race and culture. Independent even of history. Only then will one be able to acquire a fresh perspective on what is involved.

Further, moral assertions regarding whether an identity is making better or worse choices are not required. Rejecting a moralising position helps achieve the required dispassionate perspective.

To repeat: One needs to appreciate that enhancing identity with the ultimate goal of attaining wisdom is a process that occurs independent of morality. Discarding moral judgement offers an opportunity to give measured regard to the costs and benefits of life choices and actions, without needing to identify them as good or bad and so as valuable or a waste of time. All experiences are valuable. None are a waste of time. Human beings learn from every situation and experience. Indeed, people often learn more from mistakes than they do from successes. Successes reinforce that what is being done is working; mistakes and failures show up weaknesses that need to be processed and corrected.

Therefore, from a developmental perspective, rather than adopting the simplistic dichotomy of either/or and assuming one has to choose between them, it is more beneficial to invoke the principle of yin and yang, and to appreciate that both realms need to be explored at various times. The process of immersing oneself in human social environments, which offer expansive and exhausting opportunities, and afterwards evaluating the resulting experiences, is used to enrich permanent identity.

Returning, then, to the simplest view, we may regard human development as an adventure in the time-dominated physical realm, which provides opportunities to acquire information that is not available elsewhere. The result is an adventure that is rich, complex, nuanced, and—inescapably—fatal. What survives is the acquired information. Processing that information is the responsibility of the enduring identity, which is amplified and enhanced by its adventure.

Features of this teaching

Having established, in broad terms, the basis of our view of wisdom, and clarified that its acquisition is grounded in embodiment, before we go on to discuss this perspective in greater detail, we will extract from what we have just asserted a number of key axioms that underpin our position:

1. There is a realm of existence that is spiritual.
2. It is predecessor to the physical.
3. It conditions the physical.
4. The particular characteristics of physical existence on this planet offer an opportunity
5. for identities in the aforementioned spiritual realm
6. to see embodiment here as a useful means
7. to efficiently transform themselves
8. in whichever ways they wish to pursue
9. to achieve optimum identity development.

Therefore, embodiment is primarily viewed as a spiritual opportunity, which each individual uses to develop a permanent identity that consists of favourable characteristics, in fact, essential characteristics, nurtured in their own interests.

Given this, longstanding contrary views, generated by individuals whose perceptions are blinkered due to their exclusive focus on the physical domain, actually offer no impediment to those who seek a more developed understanding. Those who choose to cast aside their blinkers, to use that metaphor, open themselves to acquiring an understanding of the deeper purpose of the entire physical construct. Or, at least, of the extent to which the physical realm offers an opportunity for their permanent identity to enhance itself.

The fact that only a percentage of individuals are ready or willing to see value in this broader understanding is of no consequence whatsoever. There are many contrary beliefs, and part of the task of development is to become astute in evaluating various competing belief systems.

Acquiring discernment is one of the essential characteristics identity needs in order to develop. Being able to evaluate belief systems and appreciate the extent to which they are supported or unsupported, comes through practice.

The ability to weigh competing claims and counter claims, to reach certainty on the basis of available evidence, and so to decide which beliefs resonate with one and which do not, is a function of the depth of one's identity. Individuals need to learn to identify the different levels of their embodied identity, and to appreciate which level, superficial or deep, is resonating with whichever person or situation they encounter. Appreciating that one has different levels of identity makes it easier to select and engage with subtler and deeper internal resonances, and to separate them from attractive yet superficial socially sanctioned impulses and doctrines. Learning inner discernment is also a matter of practice.

This makes acquiring the practice of outwardly directed evaluation and inward self-discernment an essential aspect of personal spiritual development. It is a task eventually undertaken by all travellers who venture into any physical domain.

The development of levels may also be discerned historically, within cultures, in the deeper or more superficial protocols they provide to their people. However, given we are proposing this as a steady state[3] teaching, it isn't appropriate for us to offer an analysis of historical development on the basis of time, but rather to examine it on the basis of population. Accordingly, we prefer parameters that do not significantly change over time for populations, but do significantly change across the spectrum of individuals who choose to be embodied here.[4] That spectrum ranges from the inexperienced to the experienced.

Over the millennia, the few whose experiences are embedded in historical records established a number of religious traditions. Through these

---

[3] The term "steady state" refers to a system that as a whole remains the same, even though elements are changing within it. For example, a pond remains in a steady state when the water going out is matched by the water coming in: the water molecules change, but the pond level remains in a steady state. In the context here, steady state refers to the overall population of embodied human beings. There is constant flux of individuals being born and dying, but the overall population remains steady. This is so even though the human population has doubled over the last century, as an individual identity's body dies, another enters a body, creating a steady stream of exits and entrances. Just as a pond's level may go up and down over time, yet remain steady at each level, so with human population levels. The rapid doubling of the human population over the last century is negligible in both the context of a million years and in the numbers of identities co-associating with physical creatures and plants on this planet.

[4] This means that the analysis offered here is deliberately not an historical examination of changes through different eras, but instead focuses on the psychospiritual changes within an individual identity as it progresses life after life.

they have influenced followers down the centuries. Yet, as is clear to those with even a small degree of discernment, individuals who superficially align themselves with their culture's religious doctrines often only pay lip service to those doctrines, essentially living as they please. And what pleases them includes attitudes and behaviour that are completely at odds with the understanding espoused within their socially indoctrinated beliefs. It has long been this way and will long continue to be so.

In terms of categories of spiritual levels distributed through varied human cultures, we may broadly discern three. First, spiritually immature individuals usually live invisibly in their culture, that is, in terms of spiritual understanding. Second, a more thoughtful group is distributed more or less uniformly among the conformists in any religious grouping. And third, the spiritually experienced few are distributed at their culture's margins, intent on utilising their deep nature to confer directly with themselves, and with those who exist beyond them. The latter include identities such as we represent, those who are no longer part of the human domain, although they have been.

Wisdom is perennially present

Wisdom has been called perennial. It has certainly been perennially present within human communities. So this book is not the first attempt to discuss its value; throughout history there have been many others. Nor is this the only contemporary attempt, for we are addressing other groups. Neither is this the only approach conceptually, because other identities like us, that is, other reunited reintegrated nodes of Dao-consciousness,[5] are addressing a range of people across this planet's human community.

---

[5] This terminology comes from the mentors. Dao-consciousness is the undifferentiated, unmanifest consciousness that manifested everything that exists. A node of Dao-consciousness is an individual identity that is cast out of the Dao. (The idea of casting comes from the Michael Teachings.) After being cast out of the Dao some nodes fragment. Each fragment possesses individual identity. Individual human beings are fragments of a much larger node. After completing their cycles of embodiment the individual fragments reintegrate to reform their original node. For more detail see *Learning Who You Are* and *The Kosmic Web*.

Our intention is to contribute to this activity by projecting into the wider human community a refreshed perspective and set of concepts that, we hope, will stimulate a renewed appreciation of the phenomenon of human existence and its place within all life on this planet.

(That is not to demean the status of life *off* this planet, which has its own complexities. Doing so would be ludicrous. The difficulty, for human beings, is accessing that life. The appropriate attitude to address life external to this planet is on the basis of an optimal awareness of life on this planet. That requires coming to regard all components of biological life with equal care, respect, honour and intent to conserve. Because if that is not addressed first, then when encountering other life forms the naked animal fear of the unknown "other" will likely generate a feeling of being threatened, which would lead to antagonism and conflict. As a response to unknown life forms, that would be absurd.)

Continuing our attempt to stimulate a refined re-specification of life on this planet, we conclude this opening chapter with the following observations.

Over recent decades we have provided a framework of understanding that details a developmental path for every identity cast from the Dao. Embodiment is selected by individuals because it offers a highly effective way of acquiring information and freedom. And freedom *through* information. This last is the case because freedom results from enormous ordered sets of information being internalised, sorted and ordered.[6] The procedures for doing so are natural and automatic. That means techniques to enhance the process are unnecessary.

Selecting an appropriate life form, and committing to sequential embodiment in that life form, leads to the individual encountering all the complexities of life, including birth, infancy, maturation and death. The recycling of the information accumulated life by life leads to the acquisition of understanding, which in turn enables each individual to mature as a spiritual identity.

---

[6] After an individual's body dies, everything experienced and done during that life becomes information that is uploaded to the individual's spiritual identity. This information is processed between lives and used when planning the next life.

However, what we have not identified so far is the level of consciousness required for the indwelling identity to intentionally facilitate this procedure. The attribute normally ascribed to a mature level of conscious awareness is wisdom.

Acquiring wisdom depends on other contributing factors. Contemplating wisdom as a self-assigned topic requires detachment from certain factors usually considered central to human existence, such as reproduction. Those few individuals who eschew reproduction in favour of consciously collating their multi-life experience[7] have the opportunity to preselect those strands of thought they find attractive, and to recollect and process experiences not just from the current life, but memories of incidents from other lifetimes that are triggered into their awareness. Normally, it takes a specific trigger. Such alternative experience can be directly accessed by a variety of techniques other than triggered awareness. However, "stumbling across" anomalous experiences provides the most powerful stimulus to do so.

At this time in human history, given the generic international denial of spiritual identity as a real phenomenon, it is nonetheless obvious, at a deeper level of understanding, that the complexity of any individual human life exceeds its current life inputs. There is more going on inside any individual existentially and psychologically—if one cares to look—than can be explained solely by references to genes, upbringing and socialisation. Furthermore, the echoes and correspondences of everyday experience provides a halo of referencing[8] that can bring within reach sets of concepts adequate to explain present experience.[9]

---

[7] This is after having already experienced all that is involved in reproduction in prior lifetimes and likely doing so again in subsequent lives.

[8] The term "halo" is intended here to refer to a surrounding mesh of association, rather than anything traditionally religious.

[9] This final sentence is returning to the previous paragraph's theme of triggers. It is stating that our everyday experiences contain "echoes and correspondences" of prior life experiences. These provide a "halo of referencing" which, if we are sufficiently aware, we can use to explain why certain things are happening in our life, why we meet certain significant people at crucial times, and why the course of our life takes the course it does. *Practical Spirituality* and *Psychological Spirituality* discuss this in detail.

CHAPTER 2

The Field of First Cause

The dynamic of emergent identity

The parameters of human existence having been succinctly but adequately described in the preceding chapter, we now move on to describe what we are calling "the field of first cause".[1] We wish to make a number of comments in reference to its structure.

From the human perspective, the field of first cause is structureless. This results in an issue of scale similar to that of attempting to observe the physical universe using the unaided eye. In ideal viewing conditions the unaided eye sees stars and galaxies more or less uniformly distributed across the sky. However, using a sufficiently powerful telescope reveals variations in density, indicating regions of greater and lesser star populations. Very powerful telescopes, such as Hubble, show the by-now familiar imagery of very large-scale cloud-like structures. That is paralleled by a non-uniformity of distribution in the field of first cause.

We recognise that introducing the idea of structural variance within the field can only ever be considered theoretically by those living on this planet, because there is no way an embodied human being can directly perceive non-uniformity on the scale we are describing. If an embodied individual, of whatever identity and level of awareness, perceives the field of first cause at all, they perceive it as uniform. Nevertheless, it is the case

---

[1] The spiritual domain, where identities dwell. Also called Dao-consciousness.

that non-uniformity radiates into the field of first cause. So out of sight, as it were, in the deepest regions of this theoretically uniform field, there is non-uniformity.

The term "local uniformity" adequately describes the field of first cause as human beings perceive it. We use the phrase "non-local non-uniformity" to refer to the source of perturbations that affect localised regions within the field of first cause. These perturbations are related to ideas presented elsewhere, that the field of existence contains the *observer* and multiple universes.[2]

We acknowledge that explanation is an example of anthropomorphic projection, insofar as it involves inferring a distant will influences localised regions of the field of first cause. In fact, any such influence is more remote than that. Because it transcends ideation—being essentially random, abstract and beyond analysis—it is best to characterise it as impenetrable to the human intellect.

Nevertheless, we wish to make the point that it is possible for a radiative random non-uniform stimulus to generate dynamic variation in a localised region of the field. The resulting perturbation deflects uniformity away from a zero value just enough to bring about the possibility of change. When several of these random waves combine, they force a local concentration in the field sufficiently powerful to generate a self-sustaining accretion of density.[3] That accretion gives rise to individual identity.

How does this occur? Consciousness is one of the attributes present in the field of first cause, so when it is concentrated into a sufficiently dense self-sustaining accretion, self-awareness emerges. For that accretion, the distinction between what comprises identity, and what is apparently not identity, establishes a boundary in awareness. In this way condensed awareness becomes aware it is an individual identity.

For the newly condensed awareness, the path beyond that point is not determined. Time is absent. Nevertheless, this process results in a definable "something" being derived from uniformity. Thus a life begins.

---

[2] This refers to ideas introduced in *The Matapaua Conversations*, and to a vision Peter had of the multiverse. The mentors' comments relevant to this point, and a description of Peter's vision, are reproduced in Appendix 3.

[3] The accretion is called a node of Dao-consciousness in the preceding chapter.

Endless options confront the new awareness. Having not yet encountered the realm of time, developmental possibilities have no meaning. And yet change has been instigated and continues. This is the paradox of being and becoming.

We stress that, as far as the human mind is concerned, the process of identity formation has neither beginning nor end. It is a given. It can be thought of as a constant. Therefore there is no possibility of considering a limit to identity. It is a continuum that involves a constant arising of new possibility. But, of course, while dynamics are constant on the massed level, constancy does not apply to any single identity's potential.

As we have described elsewhere,[4] each identity selects opportunities from the range of possibilities available to it. Some individuals elect to associate with the physical domain. Of that set, an infinitesimal number elect to explore the possibilities available on this planet. An even smaller subset of those identities elect to co-associate with the human species.

It is impossible to calculate the total number of identities co-associating with biological species and physical processes on this planet. However, the numbers of identities co-associating with human bodies can and are counted. Of course, what is obscured by any arbitrarily imposed "head count" is that each identity selects multiple bodies to occupy over an extended period of time, and not necessarily in a linear series.

Identities cycle through human bodies, gaining experience, which leads them to enhance their identity. The same process is followed by identities of all kinds, who associate with the physical realm in myriad ways. The process of embodiment adopted by those who co-associate with the human species, in which one identity inhabits one body for the period of its lifetime, is far from universal. Other ways of connecting to the physical exist. These are discussed elsewhere, so we won't repeat them here.[5]

Hence, from remote beginnings, identity emerges by exploiting the human form. Its remote end comes when it is re-absorbed into the field of first cause, carrying with it all its combined information and constructed knowledge. It is neither possible nor relevant to offer any further detail on what that end process involves.

[4,5] See *The Kosmic Web* and *Learning Who You Are.*

Essentially, then, identity arises, undergoes an extended developmental process in the physical domain, whether by co-associating with the human species or any other, then vanishes from awareness. It doesn't vanish from itself, merely from the fields of awareness of currently embodied individuals. It may subsequently re-enter fields of awareness accessed by embodied human beings, and occasionally chooses to do so. In which case, it selects one or more embodied individuals as the targets of its communications. Such is the case here. This communication is always for a specific purpose, and is motivated by love.[6]

Freedom and consequence

Initiation into adulthood depends on completing the variety of developmental tasks normally called "growing up". These begin with being mothered, which implies receiving nurture in the form of breast milk, then prepared food. Ideally, it also involves affection, loving contact and warm embraces, which generate an identity anchored in a familiar context who feels supported and safe.

Reaching the status of adult is a widely acknowledged transition, when forgiveness for ignorant transgressions, usually accorded immature identities, ceases. Adults are considered to be self-responsible, and rightly so, for they pay with loss of freedom or loss of life should they profoundly transgress societal rules. It does not matter in the slightest exactly what those societal rules are. But to be seen to have transgressed earns them appropriate consequences and condemnation.

To the conformist, no penalties are applied. To the non-conformist, penalties depend on the severity of transgression. These two possible divergent outcomes are reinforced in the growing young via social conditioning as they progress physically and mentally towards adulthood. Conditioning contextualises attitudes and reinforces the consequences of actions. The overall impetus is to encourage growing individuals to comply with social norms.

---

[6] Having finished channelling this section, Peter comments: "Mmm, goodness me. That was quite a trip! To the furthest reaches of beginning."

Yet those norms do not apply equally to everyone. Special sanctions allow some to engage in what would otherwise be considered abnormal behaviour. These are individuals trained for the purpose of enforcing societal control. They are licensed to constrain members of a population, in some circumstances even to kill them. Like all good things, too much license can be harmful. And excessive constraint on a population inevitably engenders resistance and non-compliance. As a counterbalance, the special license granted those who force others to comply is itself transferable and may be taken away from any who exceed their mandate.

In the field of first cause none of this is either required or applies. There is full freedom to act, because every act is intentional, and every act generates information that may be processed into knowledge.

The paradox is that the field of first cause is co-substantial with, and fully interpenetrates, many other domains, including the physical. This means that full freedom to act without restraint just as logically applies while an identity is embodied as when its awareness is not confined to a physical body nor constrained by socially constructed limits.

Accordingly, social limits of all kinds may legitimately be pushed against and transgressed. Actions that constrain others, actions performed in defiance of others' preferences, and actions that explore ill-will as much as generosity, are all valuable to individuals developing understanding. This includes ignoring morality, acting in defiance of cultural and religious norms, exploring loss (via self-destructive behaviours) and causing loss to others, denying everything and nothing, and causing and experiencing death of any and all kinds. No limits are placed on the freedom enjoyed by those existing within the field of first cause.

Why have social limitations, then? And why should embodied individuals allow themselves to be constrained by them? The answer is that doing so benefits the developing identity. Cultures have accumulated the wisdom—initially drawn from observation, subsequently collected, processed and stored in written form—that some kinds of behaviour are better than others. Better, that is, in the sense that they lay foundations conducive to future development. Thus it benefits the growing young person for injunctions to be given urging them to behave in this way instead of that, and to adopt this attitude instead of some contrary attitude.

In human societies accumulated cultural wisdom, which places constraints on each individual's freedom for the benefit of both the individual and everyone else, is necessarily accorded great privilege. It is encoded into education with the aim of fashioning individuals who are able to act cooperatively; even, at the highest level, to be motivated by love. Of course, this is contrary to the natural human impulse, which emphasises benefits derived from seeking and attaining power. Especially power over others.

The resulting competition for what is conventionally termed the "hearts and minds" of individuals who comprise a society that considers itself civilised, and that accordingly promotes a set of values that could be termed "higher" over those that are "lower", is clearly desirable.

Nonetheless, the attempt to instill social norms doesn't prevent many individuals from asserting their will over others. These wilful individuals quite deliberately adopt an attitude that could be characterised as "to hell with the consequences", and use the social and psychological skills they have acquired over the course of previous incarnations to explore values and activities shunned by the majority, who endorse rational and civilised cultural conformity.

The consequences of socially better and worse behaviour, and better and worse consequences, have been laboriously weighed and recorded in culture after culture. They have been converted into prohibitions and laws that seek to limit bad behaviour. They have been incorporated into education to invite individuals to engage in best behaviour. We don't need to belabour the point any further. It is sufficient say: These issues are well-known, having reliably predictable consequences that have long been documented across multiple cultures through the eons.

Our contribution here is merely to assert that, nonetheless, it is legitimate for every individual to explore any and all options, and so learn at first hand the costs and benefits of adhering to or transgressing limits across the entire spectra of human behaviour. Indeed, having the freedom to do so is essential, because it leads to the acquisition of understanding.

As each life ends, and an identity detaches from its physical form, it carries with it the information accumulated during that life. This "precious cargo", as it might be called, is added to a repository existing at the higher spiritual self level. There the newly acquired information is processed into complex understanding. That understanding is an accumulation of all the data derived from each incarnation. Every subtle detail is transported—a process which, we note, is now on record, having been described in numerous cases of near-death experience.

Each individual's accumulated understanding, collected from each life, forms a rich and voluminous record, which is then available for the individual to draw on during any lifetime—once, that is, they become connected to their own history. It is obvious, therefore, that any individual who has such a connection is likely to be judged wiser by others in their community than an individual who is disconnected from their own bountiful record.

This is a fundamental reason for the now near-universal recognition of the value of spending time focused inwardly, precisely because it fosters such a connection. This is counter-balanced by a near-universal lack of recognition of the purpose of such a connection, which is that it offers a way to understand the extent to which one's own multi-life history contributes to one's current life. There is one further advantage to coming to understand oneself more deeply: it facilitates a deeper understanding of others.

It is obvious that the denial of spiritual existence now prevalent within the education systems of most countries actively repudiates the possibility of the deep connection we are discussing. In spite of that, individuals are free to make their own decisions and conclusions regarding the advantages of becoming intrinsically well-connected to their own multi-life history, and fostering that connection to their own and others' benefit.

CHAPTER 3

Modelling a multi-life journey

Delineating spiritual space

Here we introduce the idea that the development that results from human embodiment on this planet may be modelled.

We begin our explanation by introducing the concept of spiritual space. This is what is perceived during meditation as an expansive, unmodulated and undelineated space, putatively called the Void. It is the open blank space meditators first encounter when they begin a meditation practice. It is not that nothing or no one else is present. It is just that the beginner meditator's perception is not yet sufficiently sensitised to make subtle spiritual level perceptions. Physical perceptions, made via the body's senses, are immediate and vivid. But they are coarse in comparison to spiritual perceptions, which occur energetically, are perceived via the higher faculties, and are almost invariably faint and delicate. Through the practice of tuning one's awareness, these subtle signals may be perceived more strongly. To describe this process in scientific terms, by turning up the dial of your perception the amplitude of spiritual level perception is widened, and it becomes easier to perceive subtle signals.

This, then, provides an initial notion of what constitutes spiritual space at the lower level perceived by the embodied human being. It is an undifferentiated Void.

Now picture a vast cube. Imagine you are unable to see the cube's limits. It has limits, but they are far beyond the reach of your perception.

Modelling a Multi-Life Journey   41

Within the space delineated by this enormous cube is the same spiritual space that we have just defined. It, too, is a featureless Void.

To reinforce this conceptual shift: That vast space isn't like the space you perceive on the everyday level. It isn't space as it exists within the walls of a room in a typical human house. Nor is it space as it exists in the exponentially larger volume of an aircraft hangar. Nor is it like space in a hypothetical stadium so expansive you can't see its far walls. However, this final example delineates a space that, despite its vastness, perceptually you instinctively situate yourself at the centre of it. Your body standing in the vast space is your natural human perceptual focal point, from which you look out at what surrounds you. You sense you are in the middle, and that the stadium's space extends out from you.

Now, picture a space in which there isn't one body as a focal point. Stand back, decouple your perception from your personal physical self, and take a detached view. You are now a long way back, looking from outside the transparent walls of the unimaginably vast cube. Inside the cube is the Void. But now it is not entirely featureless. Now you can perceive an arc curving through one portion of the space. Along the arc are positioned hundreds of points. Each point is a lifetime. So the arc traces the developmental journey you make, life after life, as you experience consecutive human embodiment.

This is what we will use to model and so further discuss the nature of human embodiment and the acquisition of wisdom. Having, we hope, generated a strong image in your mind, we now detail the implications.

Locating identity in spiritual space

We have established the concept of spiritual space that is nominally bounded by a cube of unimaginable scale. Effectively, from the embodied human perspective, this is a space that is unlimited. In the space is an arc. We use the term "arc" to represent a curvilinear bisecting element within the nominal cube. We define this arc as an arc of becoming. Its location can be mapped, along with any change of its location, using the relation $E_s = ha^2$. We will return to this formula shortly. First we will further detail our model of spiritual space.

We are calling this a space, because a space is easily conceived by those we are addressing. An unbounded cube filled with limitless space may easily be pictured as an extension of the everyday examples just offered, particularly that of a vast stadium. However, in one sense they are poor analogues to the space under discussion, resulting in this notion of space needing to be viewed not literally, but as a metaphor. That is because the transition recorded by the arc is one of frequency, not distance.

We are confronted with the difficulty facing anyone trying to visualize, feel or contemplate change in frequency. This impedes our efforts as we seek to shift our space metaphor from the mental realm to the phenomenal realm, given what we are attempting to describe is an actual spiritual phenomenon. Nonetheless, these are the tools at hand.

Frequency is well established in the science community.[1] It may be measured in a range of contexts. We offer one example situation, that it results when a physical object is manipulated by a mechanically applied force so it starts moving in an oscillatory action. Geometrically, the oscillation may occur perpendicularly to the plane, parallel to the plane in one direction or another, or in circular fashion in relation to the plane. The oscillation produces resonance, which a machine may record directly by measuring the amplitude of the vibration, or the ear may hear indirectly, due to the oscillation generating a vibration that transmits energy as sound. This spectrum of frequency, and the variety of locations within the spectrum of oscillation, from minimum to maximum amplitude, can be apprehended as sound, or else plotted on a graph, the latter recording the full range of oscillating movement.

We may now apply this model to shamanic space,[2] within which varying frequency may be used to determine an individual's location, and to describe certain tendencies that affect the individual's intrinsic nature.

---

[1] Frequency (noun). 1. (General meaning) The rate at which something occurs over a particular period of time or in a given sample, i.e. the fact or state of being frequent or happening often. 2. (Scientific meaning) The rate per second of a vibration constituting a wave, either in a material (as in sound waves), or in an electromagnetic field (as in radio waves and light), i.e. the particular waveband at which radio signals are broadcast or transmitted.

[2] Shamanic space is defined here the personal experience of spiritual space. "In an-

Furthermore, the varying frequency can be plotted on a graph, and so given meaning.

In doing so, we wish to describe an individual's location as a condition of natural resonance, and to determine that location within our putative model of spiritual space. This is feasible because an individual with a sufficiently refined, focused and still awareness is able to distinguish their position in that frequency-space. It is certainly a subtle perception. Nonetheless, it is available to dedicated individuals. Furthermore, by attending to the subtle vibrations the meditator senses, it is possible to observe the presence, absence and relative location of any other identity present nearby, as well as to determine its nature. Mapped into the Void, these observations form the substance of this part of our discussion.

Behind this model is a body of work we term Agapé Theory. It has been developed in conjunction with Peter Calvert. It responds to his experiences as a meditator, and is intended to add meaning to what he has encountered. As such, Agapé Theory was originally constructed to contextualise one individual's experiences and explain the range of spiritual phenomena he has encountered. However, it has sufficient relevance to the wider population that we consider it is worthwhile expanding its original concepts. That intention has led to the creation of this short text on wisdom, which is intended to sit beside the other texts that consider the implications of Agapé Theory.[3]

We appreciate that the technical approach that drives Agapé Theory makes it inappropriate for many spiritual seekers. It will appeal to only a few. However, much in the realm of human activities — brain surgery, space flight, deep sea diving — is only pursued by a few. Rarefied specialisation doesn't lessen the value of what specialists do. Similarly, while Agapé

---

cient times meditators were known as shamans. The act of meditation, during which an embodied individual's awareness explored spiritual space, was called shamanic flight. In order to ground this discussion in human experience, and to show that what we are discussing is by no means new but has been practised throughout human history, we will use the terms shamanic space and shamanic flight. As we have repeated throughout this text, it is our terms and descriptions that are new. The experiences are not."—*The Kosmic Web*, p 110.

[3] This theory and its implications is explored in depth in *Agapé Theory*.

Theory is at the very arcane end of the spectrum of spiritual exploration, we intend it to be of use to a dedicated handful in future times. And it has a significant advantage. This is that while it will be read as abstract, even over-intellectualised, by some, its concepts are grounded in Peter Calvert's actual experience. So when others enter the same experiential space, the ideas we are offering here will be read as germane and not arcane.

This value derives from the way that Agapé Theory provides both a theoretical and an actually already experienced background to personal exploration. It offers a way to conceptualise what is experienced, and so to expand one's knowledge of what is involved. To summarise: Agapé Theory provides a conceptual framework, and models derived from that framework, useful for mapping an identity's development.

Making choices produces location change

One other essential aspect is the impact of what we choose to call consequences of choice, left and right. Whenever an identity is within the curvilinear space we are discussing, a choice becomes apparent. It is not intrinsic to the individual and their location but is rather tangential to it. It is an invitation to make a righteous choice or a "leftish" choice, as we are choosing to name it.

Clearly, this choice is apparent in long-established descriptions of spiritual knowledge and discussions of utilising it for good or ill. We prefer to adopt a geometric approach when describing this choice, as involving a decision to move towards order or towards chaos, each choice generating an incremental change in the individual's location in curvilinear spiritual space. The consequence of a single such choice results in an infinitesimal change in location. In the one thousand lifetime model we propose, movement is made towards or away from order, depending on the decision made.

Another way of conceiving this contrast is in the choice made for love or for power. Given the number of decisions made in any single life, the statistical variance can accumulate in one direction or the other, resulting, at the end of a life, in a stepwise progression in level, consisting of one or two steps. That progression may be an increment, a decrement, or zero.

Accordingly, this dynamic progression is a product of each lifetime's experience. It affects location at the spiritual identity level, determining location in the developmental arc through spiritual space. We can now assert that this location is represented by the formula $Es = ha^2$, where:

Es = spiritual energy
h = hierarchy[5]
a = agapé

These values may be represented visually, using the cube model. The purpose of this graphic is to provide a conceptual model that adequately describes the developmental arc of the human identity on the purely spiritual level. It indicates an identity's innate nature and tendencies, and the maturation process it follows as it develops from a naive node of Dao-consciousness freshly "cast from the Dao". After being projected into existence as a result of its accretion out of the apparently uniform field of first cause, it makes stepwise progress to a different level in that field. It obtains its different status as a result of collecting experience and collating it into knowledge. New opportunities then become available for its further progression.

To summarise that progress: An identity incarnates again and again in embodied form, during which it undergoes many kinds of experience. At the end of each life it archives its experiences at the higher self level, and it repeats the process however many times it needs to extract the knowledge it aims to obtain and to forge an identity that possesses a loving nature.

Because the path each individual traces is a product of their particular series of decisions, no path may be exactly predicted. Each is unique. Nonetheless, a general tendency can be mapped, proceeding from least experience to sufficient experience, which culminates in the individual no longer incarnating on this planet. That progress is represented within the

---

[5] "Willingness to act from agapé [detached spiritual love] produces hierarchy. Hierarchy constitutes the sum and product of loving acts enacted throughout a life. It is usually added up at the end of a life, which is the reason movement in hierarchy is most often assigned at the end of an incarnation—although some rare individuals may carry out loving acts of such power that their hierarchy is raised while still embodied." *The Kosmic Web*, p 106

cube model as rising through the following values: hierarchy = 0 to 100, agapé frequency units = 25,000 to 35,000, willingness to bequest agapé = 41,000 to 45,000.

The units are not to be understood literally. They are meaningful only within the terms of this model, which is a mental model designed to describe otherwise obscure reality. As such, it is a simplification of what is involved, our intention being to offer a comprehensible (rather than comprehensive) representation of the developmental arc human beings follow as they transition from naive to wise.

Clearly, this model echoes other historical attempts to describe the meaning and purpose of human life. We are not claiming that the developmental path thus mapped is more desirable than any other path followed by other nodes of Dao-consciousness. We merely assert that it happens. We also remind our readers that this path is outside time, so there is no way the embodied can influence the rate of transition. But if anyone impartially appraises their stage and state using the three values, they may ascertain their probable current position within their overall developmental arc.

By implication, one may also observe others' behaviour, attitudes, values and innate qualities, and as a consequence conclude that they are at a different location in the developmental arc from oneself. It is imperative not to regard one individual as better or worse than another, for all identities are equal on this developmental path, both at its outset and at the point of transition beyond it. We also emphasise that this process has nothing to do with social hierarchy, which is a separate issue entirely.

This model is our attempt to foster an understanding of how, at a core level, one person potentially differs from another during incarnation. Commonly, these distinctions are only perceived when people are under duress, during periods of extreme social upheaval, when their "steadiness under fire", to use that military metaphor, becomes apparent. The imperturbability displayed by the experienced identity is naturally an attribute possessed by only a small portion of incarnated humanity.

CHAPTER 4

Balance and Serenity

[From Peter's journal]
Yesterday I had a conversation with my co-meditator, sharing our intentions for the coming year. Near its end I felt discomfort due to the quality of the emotional link engendered by our talk, and was slightly abrupt in terminating our otherwise enjoyable discussion. She had been describing a lack of clarity in her plans, that she felt some confusion, and that she would wait until clarity came before committing to any particular course of action.

I subsequently had the sense a dark net of confusion was enveloping me, so worked to disconnect from it through auric cleansing. That was quickly successful, bringing me back into a state of clarity and serenity. I then registered an unexpected chill and wondered if it indicated the presence of non-embodied identity and an opportunity to receive more input towards the new book. So it was.

The depth of serenity

Entering the realm of time and space is a necessary prerequisite for taking on an embodied life. But doing so does not absolve an individual of the responsibility to pay attention to the condition of their being.

That brings us to an aspect of freedom we have not yet addressed.

Previously, we discussed freedom in terms of an individual's development, and suggested it may be measured using the agapé scale.[1] We now wish to discuss freedom in relation to maintaining inner balance. Balance promotes freedom from malign influences. Balance facilitates freedom from ecstasy, with its potential for mania, which it prudently helps avoid, as well as freedom from contagion, confusion and depression, with their potential for life-ending madness.

The inner balance that situates an individual between those two extremes also involves a state of serenity. One may characterise serenity in terms of lightness or heaviness. Quiet joy associated with light serenity is its own reward. Heavy serenity carries qualities of imperturbability, and perhaps immovability, yet without any trace of darkness or turbidity.

The range of feelings available while maintaining a middle way may be contrasted with the sense of being enmeshed in a net of dark confusion, unsettled by indecision and lack of clarity, that potentially engenders the feeling of being trapped.

We mention this to bring more clarity to the options available within the realm of being. What we are drawing attention to is a condition of spiritual being that is distinct from any issues arising from embodiment. The clarity of perception an embodied individual has occasionally or more frequently, their deep insights into what is happening around them, and the serenity they sometimes experience, are conditions that derive not from the social levels of their identity, but from the spiritual levels of their being. Social interactions can add to or subtract from these qualities. That is, social circumstances may distract an individual from clarity of perception and serenity of feeling. Alternatively, an individual may be able to include clarity and serenity in their everyday social interactions. Yet those qualities remain intrinsically separate from the social level.

We emphasise this to encourage discernment, that is, for individuals to distinguish between matters concerning their being at the spiritual level and those concerning the body. We identify the physical, social, intellectual and psychological aspects of human identity as distinct and separate from the spiritual identity and its intrinsic condition. To this distinction we

---

[1] "Agapé scale" refers to the three axes defined on page 46.

add those factors pertaining to the energetic level, as they are sometimes identified [i.e., the aura]. The spiritual being is also distinct from them.

Historically, the condition of primary spiritual being has been represented in a confused manner. This is an issue because traits that are germane to the embodied identity, most of which are psychological in nature, with some physiological, have been ascribed to the spiritual self, while qualities that are germane to the spiritual identity have been mistakenly ascribed to the embodied identity.

In this text we use the terminology of "spiritual existence", "being", which is spiritual, and "identity", which for human beings exists on two primary levels, ephemeral embodied identity and original non-embodied identity. There is an overlap between embodied human identity and spiritual identity, insofar as an upcoming life is shaped according to the spiritual identity's intention. It embeds in its embodied human identity certain qualities and traits that it wishes to work with during its next incarnation. Nonetheless, a distinction needs to be made between these two fundamental levels of identity.

To facilitate this distinction, and in an attempt to anchor human existence to conditions set by primary spiritual being, we have originated an appropriate nomenclature, such as the field of first cause. Naturally, the sense of identity within the field of first cause never changes, even while an individual's locus of identity habitually fluctuates in and out of embodiment, and despite all the psychological, social and bodily inputs that demand the individual pay attention to them.

The ultimate challenge in every lifetime, then, is to differentiate between what is involved in attending externally, attending internally, and recovering the sense of original identity as it stands in the field of first cause. We note that is the intention behind the ancient injunction, "Know yourself".[2]

A tool that facilitates differentiation is insight meditation. An exemplary example is Vipassana meditative practice.[3] This practice offers a way

---

[2] From the Greek, *gnōthi sauton*. The maxim was inscribed in the Temple of Apollo, situated in Delphi.
[3] Vipassana is an ancient meditation practice that goes back to the time of the Buddha. Today ten-day courses are taught in various places around the world.

to identify the different levels of existence, and to learn to give attention to each level, no matter whether contrived or controlled. It helps a meditator develop the skill to distinguish between embodiment and its issues on the one hand, and original identity and its intention on the other. This same goal is shared by every multi-layered model of embodied existence created throughout human history, in culture after culture. These models, whether conceived in the context of religious belief, or empirically, via the self-observational practices of early science, were all devised to understand the full breadth and depth of what is involved in being human. They all share the aim of recognising the human identity in terms of its continuous existence, in contrast to its doings during embodiment.

We celebrate the intention to inhabit the condition of serenity as first preference. From that location within identity all other levels may be seen in full clarity, notwithstanding the distractions that naturally accompany embodiment. From that location we all show love.

An impediment to serenity

> [From Peter's journal]
>
> An image appeared in my mind to accompany this download, in support of its description. The image reminded me of the Jewish mystic visual concept of the Kabbalah. It had a strong central column, indicating primary being, and grouped around it were various clusters representing the factors associated with secondary being, its qualities and relations.[4]
>
> What was clear to me from the image is that the levels represented connections at various heights on the central column, and that one could freely move on that axis of intrinsic identity.

---

[4] The image is of the Sefirot. It models the emanations of Ein Sof (the Infinite), which it manifested in the process of generating the world. The manifestations number ten. They are traditionally drawn in three vertical lines. The central vertical consists of four emanations, while the left and right verticals contain three each. This concept of emanations echoes Plato's notion of the One emanating the eternal Forms. The central column of the Sefirot, which has Keter (crown) at the top and Yesod (Foundation) towards the bottom, also suggests the chakras and kundalini.

[Later] I have been shown another image. It is somewhat abstract, of the dantian[5] surrounded by thorns. I have the sense it's a self-portrait. And it was accompanied by a voice, "I can't do this alone! They can't do this without me!"

The reason they have shown me the dantien shrouded by thorns is because it constitutes a problem! It's not a random illustration, it's illustrating a specific impediment, therefore it needs to be taken seriously. I've been hiding in eating and reading and sleeping, but it is important to face this.

[Later] I have committed to a three day fast to assist the process of clearing or releasing the characteristics that caused the self-portrait to look so thorny. In addition, there has been another statement, which appears to have emerged from my memory: "You'll never take me alive!" It indicates determination against opposition, a willingness to die rather than change. Also, I think, a willingness to go to the flames rather than be corrupted, either by adopting corrupt practices or corrupt beliefs, or by becoming part of a corrupt Catholic administration. I sense it is a memory of my experience of being a Cathar (~1200 CE).[6]

It involves, partially at least, a central determination for freedom at any price, even if only by relinquishing the current body. I wonder how that is balanced out by death by hanging, death by guillotine, death by torture, death by sword? Because

---

[5] A human identity is the fragment of a node of Dao-consciousness. In its spiritual form it may be visualised as an almost transparent sphere, with a kernel at its centre. "When the spirit sphere co-associates with a human body, the point of alignment is at what the Japanese term the hara centre, just below the belly button. Accordingly, we identify the kernel as the hara dantien. (Japanese *hara*, belly, Chinese *tan tien*, energy centre.)" *The Kosmic Web*, p 88.

[6] The Cathars, who lived in southern France and northern Spain, were part of a movement that rebelled against Catholic theology and clerical control. They called themselves Good Christians. The name Cathar is from the Greek, *katharoi* (the pure ones), and was used ironically by the Inquisitors. Cathars considered human beings reincarnated until they achieved salvation. The Catholic Church judged them heretics, and murdered thousands of them during the twelfth to fourteenth centuries.

I have another image, of being in a sword fight, and abandoning that body to death by ceasing to fend off the attack, just holding my weapons aside and allowing my body to be run through the heart, thus giving up the fight, acquiescing perhaps to what felt like the inevitable. Behind it I sense the hope of coming back in better times. Well, here I am!

So is it a habitual stance of resistance that is the impediment? Desire for supremacy? Desire to be right? Desire to impose my will and make other people change their minds? What right do I have to do any of that?

[Later] During my meditation a little while ago I seemed to be surrounded by a crowd! More and more and more came, until there was an image of hundreds of people, all at my level. The impression I had was they were all my 363 prior selves. I had the impression of a great variety of different races and dress or undress, and the idea that I needed to defend myself was diluted by the combined will to defend me—the idea that I already had a great crowd on my side. That's a very foreign feeling! But a rather comforting one. Oh, what a lot of different people I have been! But does that make any difference to my defended nature? Or bristly resistant nature? I don't seem to get any clear answer to that apart from, "No!"

CHAPTER 5

Ecstasy, Intimacy and Death

Additional parameters of love

We now introduce additional aspects to our model of spiritual development. These are intended to clarify what has been presented in the preceding chapters.

First is the capacity to move. In the lower astral[1] the capacity to move is restrained by the characteristics of the individual, rather than the characteristics of the place.

The term integral Ex[2] expresses what is involved. It is a composite term that comprises several sub-dimensions.

- The first of these is the intrinsic capacity to love, as we have previously indicated.[3]
- The second is the capacity to give out love.
- The third is the capacity to accept love.
- The fourth is the choice between intimacy and ecstasy.

---

[1] The lower astral is a subset of the astral domain. It is where human beings exist while embodied. It is identified by gray light, which gives somewhat obscured vision in the vast space commonly known as the Void.
[2] This is a function denoting incremental movement on the spiritual level that results from actions intended by agapé (love). Many actions must be integrated to create a one-step migration or incremental shift in agapé. The function is $Ex = \int Ex$.
[3] For the first three listed see *Learning Who You Are*, pp 76-89, which offers an introductory description. More detail is given in *The Kosmic Web*, pp 105-123.

We need to explain the odd choice of these terms—intimacy and ecstasy—for they do not function as simple qualities of being. Ecstasy, of course, is chosen because of its relationship with pleasure, and the capacity for pleasure to ascend through the various centres on the auric level.[4] Where ecstasy is fixed at the survival or sexual levels, it exists at a relatively low order. Higher development, or more experience, commonly increases the capacity to experience ecstasy by lifting it into the aura's higher levels. These more intense and refined ecstatic feelings reflect an individual's higher functioning.

Intimacy is the capacity to be intimate with another person, that is, to blend with the energy of another person on the auric level. An individual's capacity for intimacy is reflected in the extent to which they can freely exchange energy via the aura. (It also relates to the mind under normal circumstances, but we are limiting our comments here to the energetic level.) A fully intimate pair willingly exchanges energy on all levels. But in practice willingness to be intimate is commonly confined to the survival and sexual levels, with conflict frequently emerging at the will centre level. Thus intimacy manifests as a limited willingness to exchange energy.

The four qualities that constitute an individual's Ex condition their capacity to move in the lower astral. That is why we are associating them with the model we presented in Chapter 3, because they provide a way to appreciate the qualities specific to the non-bodily level as it functions within an ordinary embodied person. These capacities are often related to quality of mind, but they are more accurately assigned to qualities of spiritual experience, for that is where they manifest from. Our point is that the capacities for experiencing love—experiencing it, giving it out, accepting it—and for experiencing ever more refined feelings of intimacy and ecstasy, are perceived in an individual's thoughts and their emotional exchanges, but they do not originate at the mind and emotion levels.

Intimacy and giving out love

We will now discuss in more detail an individual's willingness to give out love. This is also composite in nature. It requires several preconditions.

The first of these preconditions is the capacity for intimacy. Of course, this is initially experienced during infancy. Intimacy normally and naturally develops as a result of an infant's pair-bonding with its birth mother. Conversely, its development is impaired by the birth mother's absence or when a carer replaces the birth mother. In each case, the individual's capacity for intimacy is not only diminished during childhood, but often for life. Similarly, if the birth mother suffers a traumatic event before, during or after birth, which negatively impacts her ability or willingness to be intimate, the child is most likely again affected for life. That is, unless active intervention in the form of therapy is undertaken, which results in a deep change in the person's emotional capacity.

A second factor preconditions an individual's willingness to be intimate. This occurs when an infant's reaching out is rebuffed by either the birth mother or her replacement carer. The infant's bruised feelings may be reversed in later life through therapy, but for most rejection is deeply imprinted and maintains its negative impact throughout that lifetime. This severely impacts the individual's ability, expectations and willingness regarding giving and receiving intimacy.

The third precondition is fear. We are referring to a deep tendency to be fearful, that builds up as a result of experiences accumulated life after life. Where an infant has had no experiences that have generated fear in them—an almost impossible condition, we might add—their capacity to trust anyone or anything in their proximity is uninhibited. However, it is more normally the case that they have undergone experiences that generated fear during prior lives, and as a consequence they have difficulty trusting others in this life. This deep distrust manifests in fear of strangers, fear of commitment, and fear of the new, among others.

Where fear has been experienced intensely during multiple prior lives, and little to no remediation has been undertaken at a deep level during any subsequent lives, being unwilling to trust severely inhibits an individual's capacity to be intimate. It will manifest in them during infancy and continue throughout that life.

These are the main factors that condition an individual's willingness

---

[4] This is a reference to the aura and the major chakras, which rise through the body, from the base of the spine to the top of the head.

to move in the lower astral. Significantly, these factors also condition an individual's ability to move on after their body's death.

Moving on after death

If an individual's limited capacities and self-limiting attitudes remain un-remediated, then they continue to apply at the end of that life. An individual who has low trust, high fear, an undeveloped ability to experience ecstasy, and little willingness to be intimate, is constrained in their capacity to move in the lower astral on exiting their body. Besides their inner state, two other factors impact on their capacity to move after death.

The first is the circumstance of their dying. For many, dying is a gradual process, so they have the opportunity to reconcile to their body's coming demise. But for others death comes suddenly, so they have no such preparation. For some, death comes as a complete surprise. In fact, a very small percentage has difficulty appreciating that their body has died. As a result, they hover in the lower astral, uncertain what to do next.

The second factor is an individual's beliefs regarding what follows their body's death. Most notable are their expectations regarding whether they will be rewarded or punished, whether they will go to heaven or hell, or their assumption that death is a great blank which terminates their awareness. Such beliefs limit their appreciation that they are a spiritual identity who, after their body's death, has a natural trajectory to follow.

That trajectory is into the clear light, and beyond. However, self-limiting attitudes, conditioned beliefs, and deep-seated assumptions regarding their own inner nature, may lead individuals to choose not to immediately follow their natural post-life trajectory. They are then confined to an "in between" modality, often trying to maintain a tenuous connection to the physical world, and for whatever reason—there are many—avoiding engaging with the nature of their situation. These individuals then become what we identify as lost souls.

These flexibly interacting complex factors account for the variability in post-death experience. A thorough examination of an individual's state before they begin the process of dying could give some indication of the likelihood of an easy transition. Or not. But, of course, this is never done.

And would actually be of little advantage. What is sufficient is simply to recite to the dying individual the following words.

A recitation for the dying

Recognise that you are a soul currently in the process of exiting the body. You will be set free from the constraints and limitations imposed by that body, and will be free to move at the time and in conditions of your choosing, to depart from this place and these people and return to the clear light where you belong.

The path to get there may be short or long, but it is easy if you are simple in your intention to gladly exit this place, taking with you the information you have gathered through your life here, and proceed with goodwill and love for those who remain. But do so without attachment, recognising that their task is done, as is yours, that you can take nothing with you other than your own being and all of its acquired information.

The task when you get there is to integrate that information into the being you are, then evaluate your future prospects. You will get help with this, so there no need be fearful. For you go to a safe and loving place and will always be accepted there.

Some will come to find you at the time of your departure. They will willingly guide you home to the clear light. For that is where you are going. And it will feel like coming home. Go in peace and love, and rest.

Repeating this a maximum of ten times will be sufficient to inculcate into the mind of the dying individual that relaxation into the process is their best option. They will become conscious that they are departing, and so have no expectation of staying. Or, if they do expect to stay, they will know they have a choice about how long that may be. When their unfinished business is complete, they will know on a conscious level what the next thing to do is. Knowing that will help them.

Repeating the recitation need not continue past the time of death. This is contrary to other traditions. Once an individual's body has ceased to function, the individual has already separated from it. And having heard the recitation prior to their body's demise, they do not need to hear it again. If it was not heard prior to their body's demise, then having established a connection with them, one recitation is sufficient. Where you doubt your connection with them, use your intention to re-establish a connection. A recitation of ten times is more than sufficient and need not be exceeded.

This is our specification for the practice of dying. It will be sufficient for all circumstances. We offer it with love in order to convey into the English language knowledge long garnered elsewhere.

CHAPTER 6

Negative After-life Possibilities

After-death mobility

We have more to add about willingness to move in the lower astral domain after death. In earlier chapters we dealt with the *capacity* to move in the astral domain. *Willingness* to move is first determined by becoming aware of one's condition and location. One's *freedom* and *capacity* are the next issues.

As we have already discussed, freedom to move and capacity to move come with experience. Recognition of the experience is the only potentially missing step. If one takes the trouble to inform a dying person that they are already experienced, that gives them conscious understanding, which they may then use to access their previous experience and so feel the consequent freedom. They know that they can move if they choose to move. But this also depends on them being willing to do so.

Willingness to move after the body's death relates to whether or not they have unfinished business. If there is none, if they feel complete in their aspirations for the life they just lived, and so are at peace, then they may simply leave without regret and without looking back, knowing their task is done as they planned it. If they do have unfinished business, they can attend to it promptly, understanding their condition, knowing that wherever their need takes them they can go there and complete it.

Hence being aware they have the freedom to move, that they have the capacity to move, and are willing to act, are sufficient. That is why these possibilities are included in the recitation for dying, hidden by implication, but nevertheless there.

However, lurking fear and uncertainty can overwhelm the entire process. That is the reason for the repetition. As the individual's beliefs are challenged, and if the content of the recitation is unfamiliar, then layer after layer of fear and uncertainty will become exposed as contrary to what the dying person needs. They will be released as understanding and acceptance penetrates the dying individual's mind.

If the person has already died, and they have not had the opportunity to have these ideas shared with them, then fear and uncertainty can be addressed immediately. Sharing with the person their true state and capacities can be done in one recitation.

If the person is obstinately uncooperative, or for whatever reason their mind is closed off, nothing spoken will change their situation. But for all but the most recalcitrant the recitation will be adequate.

Were this process to be adopted across the world, the number of individuals who remain close to the embodied population would progressively reduce. As a result, the world would to a degree be calmer.

The influence of the recently dead on the embodied population is actually not large, because most people are not closely attached to those who have passed, nor are they typically sensitive to post-death interference. But the percentage of individuals who can and do disturb the lives of the embodied are neither tiny nor trivial. Without putting numbers on the situation, we simply state that for the sake both of those who are exiting their lives on this planet, and for those they leave behind, reciting the advice to the dying is a recommended procedure.

The recitation also has social and familial benefits. It adds to the activity of saying goodbye, enhancing the shared emotional warmth while being of benefit to the one who is passing. It can create a memorable occasion, bringing a fractured family together, or further bonding a united family. It serves as a ritual for those who need such an activity, and is an expression of love for those who do not. It helps those who are being left behind, creating closure for themselves in their lives, as well as encouraging closure among others. The joint activity allows peace to arrive, and for it to be perceived. It positively contributes to the development of a heightened state of awareness in which those with sufficient sensitivity can see the departure of their loved one, hence building understanding of the true process of dying and departing from the body. All these will constructively contribute to a simplified and extended understanding of what happens when a spirit, the true identity, leaves its body, their adopted home.

Those who do not move on easily

We draw attention to two post-death scenarios. The first is that the majority of individuals leave their term of embodiment satisfied with their life and the progress they made during it. They feel closure and have no ongoing entanglements with those they are leaving behind. They go on their way easily, quickly, and directly to the clear light.

This state is somewhat different to the second scenario, which applies to those who are determined to be controlled by residual fear, are concerned with unfinished business, are attached to property, or have emotional entanglements of one kind or another. Some are fearful regarding their destination, of being boxed in a coffin and buried in the ground. Some fear being attacked by flesh-eating creatures, or are similarly concerned for themselves as a physical organism. This is especially so if they fully and completely identify themselves with their body. Such individuals find themselves in a state of relative ignorance, lacking clarity regarding their life purpose and their destination once their life is over. They are especially confused regarding the nature of their continuance. Hence, after their body dies they tend to stay where they are.

Some of the more extreme cases have been encountered when undertaking soul rescues.[1] One particularly appropriate case to consider is the climber who wouldn't let go because he feared he would fall and die, not realising that had already occurred.[2] This individual had a well-ordered and rational understanding of what was required for him to survive in a precarious climbing situation. His body's death made his rational understanding obsolete. He had a particularly rigid character and adhered

---

[1] A number of cases are recorded in *People of the Earth* (2019).
[2] For the full account see Appendix 4.

to a set of inflexible beliefs regarding what he had to do to survive. These factors combined to make his case unusual, and indicative of a worst-case scenario.

Not that there was malice in him. However, malice in the deceased who has not moved on can add an extra dimension to their consequent actions and how they impact on those who are still embodied. A case that illustrates this possibility is of a young English orphan. He was treated badly during his life by those who had been legally tasked with having a duty of care towards him. Their frustrations, reinforced by their limited abilities, made his life worse. They incurred his malice, and he exacted his revenge.[3]

In fact, that was a mild case. There are much more pernicious examples, however we don't wish to detail any further the negative consequences of unskillfully treating the dying or recently dead. We wish merely to point out that there can be negative consequences.

Mara and others

> [From Peter's journal]
> I seem to have in front of me a turbulent energy conveying the impression of negative intention directed in my direction. I feel fixed by a challenging stare, not malevolent exactly, but more along the lines of, "I exist. Recognise me and deal with me. Feel my reality. Quail at the sight of me!" It projects a dark, pulsing red colour, and has a truculent manner, as if it ought to have horns. It feels like it potentially has many mouths to consume whatever comes within its sphere of influence. There's a kind of a dark boiling quality to it, suggesting something like an angry bull, or a dark multi-armed warrior intent on destruction. Or a mouth equipped with large teeth capable of gnashing oneself. Yet, as an entity, it is neither pervasive nor particularly large.
>
> It steadily receded from my awareness. If I had in-built responses that triggered fear I'm sure it could have been mag-

---

[3] For details on this individual's situation see Appendix 5.

nified in my awareness. I might then have regressed into an infantile fearful state, feeling completely at its mercy.

I think of Mara, the Devil, and various dark tribal identities that could be invoked to destructively interfere with other people. The fierce warrior images in Buddhist temples in China and India. Perhaps it represents an example of the polar opposite to the exquisite event of yesterday, constituting the singularity of the positive. And yet it seems puny in comparison, significant only to the extent that it matched qualities inherent in a person's character.

I know such entities are spoken of everywhere, symbolically represented by image and thought, tradition and literature. I imagine that were a dying person surrounded by witnesses open to the approach of that quality of energy, then the collective fear could have simply made everybody run away in panic, cursing the dying one for having brought that quality of energy, or at least attributing its presence the dying person.

So although I didn't feel any fear, I recognise that others who are inexperienced may well have done so.

Spiritual retribution

Thus we show you a complementary opposite. There are others, and we will show them to you, but that is sufficient for today. These factors influence the circumstances of those who are in the process of dying, and of those who, out of social respect, accompany them during their passing. There have been situations through the millennia when a combination of fear-driven circumstances have led to outrage, social disaster, and retribution, not only physical, but also spiritual.

The concept of spiritual retribution has a long history. We will address that now, for it has led to persistent and ugly disturbances affecting embodied humanity. Along with social disruption, retribution is designed, and in some instances actually produces, the destruction of relationships. While spiritual retribution is a rare event, its very rarity leads to it being magnified by a community's mythology. As a worst-case scenario, it has no equal.

Spiritual retribution is most likely to occur at the dying of a feared and revered tribal figure, where the dying individual is generally regarded as being both powerful and manipulative. That role is commonly held by the shaman, in their negative role as sorcerer or voodoo practitioner, calling on the dark powers, as they are commonly attributed.

Willed retribution can cause great social consternation for decades, even for centuries, if memories associate a catastrophic social event with a particular individual. The possibility of that or a similar scenario becomes amplified where a population's beliefs make them susceptible to something terrible occurring which they feel powerless to avert. In that situation a combination of internal fear, an inclination to imagine the worst, and a sense of powerlessness, become a potent combination that conditions their response.

All this can result in horrible actions, which are usually directed towards the identified (or imagined) perpetrator of the process. Very often that is the person who is in the process of dying, or has died. The body of such an individual has occasionally been subjected to great disrespect, through ritual mutilation or dismemberment. The long-term fear-driven result is a widespread, troublesome disturbance that extends through a local population.

Communities without positive spiritual role models, or that carry the belief that negative role models outweigh positive role models—in terms of the ability of the supposed dead to influence the living—can be left in a very sorry state after an event such as we are describing. Fortunately, it is rare. Yet even today some groups continue to uphold those traditions.

One of the advantages of the extension of international communication systems is that it gives most people on the planet access to the wealth of information concerning the positive traditions within the world's spiritual literature. This in turn facilitates a focus on, and a preference for, loving intervention during the process of dying. Access to that information is likely to progressively eliminate, or at least drastically reduce, the probability of the kind of event we have just been describing. That will be to the benefit of the embodied population as a whole. But will take some time.

CHAPTER 7

The Complications of Dispersal

On the memory of being spirit

At this point we introduce another factor that influences individuals' ability to move on after the body dies. This is their willingness, during their life, to give credence to the memory of being spirit.

One theme persistently echoes throughout human history: that the bulk of the world population has consistently rejected the idea that they are spirit first, last and always. As applies to any other historical tendency, that rejection results from accumulated personal experience. Even where individuals' cultural beliefs lead them to accept on a theoretical level that they are spirit, limitation of perception means they invariably have no way to personally and directly verify that is the case.

Nonetheless, most individuals gradually accumulate repeated anomalous perceptions life after life—anomalous, that is, in relation to the assumption that identity is primarily physical and bodily. These perceptions occur mostly in heightened states of awareness, via meditation, prayer, trance, during religious rituals, in dreams, as a result of ingesting mind-altering plants, and after they have repeatedly witnessed and experienced bodies' deaths and sensed the presence of loved ones after they have died. Eventually, a time comes when their accumulated life experiences provide them with incontrovertible evidence that yes, they are spirit. This realisation is sufficiently powerful for them to make a permanent attitudinal shift, and to willingly grant credence to the theory that humans are spirits.

The individual through whom we speak at this time has made that transition in this lifetime. There have been other lifetimes when he has considered the possibility, and has sought evidence regarding it, but he has been relatively unsuccessful in acquiring it. In previous lives he has witnessed others transition from relative disbelief to relative certainty regarding spiritual matters. Nonetheless, a habitual resistance to accepting he is spirit has been ingrained into his identity on the spiritual level—we note the irony implicit in that statement.

The curious condition of doubt regarding one's nature is part of the reason for the general pattern of self-doubt across humanity. In our collaborator's case, he has only relatively late in this lifetime come to the conviction that his self-willed choices are a legitimate expression of his personal identity. Equally recently, he has come to indisputably appreciate that as an identity he is spirit first, foremost and always.

Yet while he has become willing to simply acquiesce to input from the spiritual level, nonetheless some long-ingrained inhibiting factors remain present. These are the source of the resistance he has recently perceived within himself. This resistance needs to be confronted. It is why he perceived the image of the dantien surrounded by dark thorns. The thorns represent the deep resistance that results in his unwillingness to accept contrary beliefs.

With that situation made clear, the opportunity is now available to reduce the inbuilt resistance. While the extensive material he has channelled over the years may give the impression that here is an individual who is endlessly willing to confront these issues, at a deep level that is not the case. There has only been a slow weakening of resistance over several decades. This is not a criticism. It is simply to describe this individual's condition, shaped as it is by personal history accumulated over many lives.

Given he has recently acquired new-found certainty concerning the spiritual nature of his identity, will that certainty persist in future lives? There is no guarantee. The resistance is long established, while the certainty is relatively new. A delicate balancing act between the two significant personality features is now in play. We require persistence of our own to address it. Nevertheless, the accumulated achievement to date is sufficient to encourage us to sustain our connection to this identity.

Avoiding enthusiastic conversion

Returning to the issue of an identity's developmental path and their manifestation not just as a spirit, but their appreciation that they *are* a spirit, we note the dissonances that arise between an individual's personally developed beliefs and beliefs developed and promulgated by others. There is nothing wrong with such clashes. In fact, they are inevitable. But they do become deadly when a majority of believers attempt to persuade others to relinquish their beliefs, and use force to do so.[1]

As we have stated elsewhere, we have no intention of proselytising. We are doing no more than presenting this example of one man's confrontation with his longstanding and persistent beliefs and using this situation as an opportunity to describe another aspect of the myriad ways spiritual life impacts on physical life.

But the fact human beings regularly force their beliefs on others leads us to draw attention to an issue relevant to this material. In the past, any new major shift in viewpoint has provided an opportunity for individuals to enthusiastically proclaim their newly acquired understanding to others.

The downside of this is that if they don't constrain their enthusiasm, and if they have an opportunity to use their new beliefs to bolster their power socially, then their proclamations become an exercise in conversion: a transition from one rigid set of beliefs, even of disbelief, to another set of rigid beliefs. There are examples throughout history.

We prefer not to do this. We are not seeking to convert readers from one set of beliefs to another. We intend only to offer these perspectives, and leave those who come across them to use them to their personal benefit as they see fit.

Nevertheless, we acknowledge that our caution has not been shared throughout human history. Instead, once an individual achieves a new level of understanding, they tend to launch themselves into proselytising to any who will listen. If they have a sufficiently charismatic personality, then others grant them the status of a purveyor of new information, new

---

[1] See Peter's journal entry on page 52, in which he refers to his experience among the Cathars and his determination not to renounce his beliefs.

inspiration, new understanding. They are lauded as a corrector of previous error, and those who seek inspiration gather around them.

We repeat, that is not our intention here. In fact, it is rather unlikely a similar result will occur in relation to this material, given the low-key manner it is being projected into the worldwide community. Further, the structures of communication that have recently become available means there is now no need to rely on the enthusiasm of individuals or their contemporaries. For our purposes, it is sufficient to utilise the information dispersal systems now established and, given our relative disregard for time, to simply allow the information to penetrate wherever it may be found acceptable. This departure from historical trajectories of information sharing is a consequence of technological developments being in place that were simply unavailable in prior centuries.

As regards specific fields for dispersal, we have striven to anchor the material to constructs of thought that are already established. They can be briefly listed as being in the fields of social humanity, anthropological humanity, psychological humanity, philosophical humanity, in the recently established field of transpersonal psychology, and in the many historically constructed concepts of spirituality, as diverse as they are across cultures. Regarding the last field, the fact that people's psychological understanding of spirituality been historically situated within religious frameworks need be no impediment at this time. Indeed, relevant insights and doctrines from diverse religious traditions can be made use of as points of similarity and contrast in order to legitimise this new delivery of refreshed understanding.

To do so, certain relevant features need to be identified and discussed, with points of agreement and disagreement mapped out in detail. We will begin that task now.

CHAPTER 8

This Perspective is Not Moralistic

Redefining self-aggrandisement

Earlier we introduced the term integral Ex[1] to mathematically describe the incremental shift that occurs between lives as an individual develops on the spiritual level. We acknowledge we offered it with a degree of wry humour, because we are perfectly well aware that the integral symbol is an elongated $\int$, indicating SUM between limits. $\int$ combined with Ex makes $\int$ Ex, which spells "sex". For human beings, sex is an exquisite driver of relationships, from which much is learned.

It is completely appropriate to consider sex a noble activity, embraced in the interests of the long-term evolution of each human being. The fact it can manifest in all kinds of other ways is neither here nor there.

The term "noble" we just used is present in the language people commonly use when they judge others as acting in the "right way", which is the opposite of the "wrong way". But deeply buried in these two phrases is a spiritual level appreciation that the purpose of incarnation is to ennoble oneself, and through one's relationships to ennoble others.

Many human relationships include invitations to sexual arousal. The gender combination is immaterial. What matters is the presence of love, respect, humour and sensitivity. This leads to sex involving ennoblement. In the highest human sense, we consider ennoblement to be the "right way".

---

[1] See p 54.

We note that sex also involves a desire for self-aggrandisement. We use this term in the very particular sense that contained within it is a recognition of the desire for expansion. Specifically, expansion into nobility. Self-aggrandisement in this sense occurs when one seeks to ennoble oneself, and in the process also ennobles others. Hence our attribution is intended to be thoroughly positive. As such, it should be sharply distinguished from the common pejorative sense.

Self-aggrandisement in our sense includes the multi-layered intention of fostering self-love and directing love to others, and being willing to act in a kindly and helpful manner towards oneself as well as towards others. Doing so is the "right way", as we are defining it here. It lays foundations for the long-term acquisition of understanding, for accumulating experience and merit, and for developing a loving nature. It leads to developing freedom to move on the spiritual level, along with willingness to move.

This outcome is directly analogous to the Buddhist precepts formulated in the Noble Eightfold Path. Ours is a modern affirmation of that path. Not that the Buddhist world requires affirmation in any sense. But the linking does offer an opportunity to show that the ancient Buddhist formulation of understanding, and the precepts offered here, share the same fundamental intent. They describe the same sets of criteria on which to build a moral life.

Judging choices wrong is not right

Morality is an issue that we have generally avoided. Our only prior formulation regarding right and wrong has been our discussion of the plane of morality,[2] as we designated it. We assigned the "right way" to the upper right quadrant of that plane, in contrast to other choices that could be made. Beyond affirming that an individual has free will to choose any option they wish, we have declined to add a moral value to any choices. This is a crucial aspect of the context we are offering here. To affirm: this is not a moralistic perspective.

Thus we consider it completely inappropriate to judge as wrong an

---

[2] See Appendix 6.

individual's choice to embrace negative experiences. In fact, it is right. It is essential. It is necessary. Because only by doing so does one acquire personally experienced certainty regarding the outcome of one's choices. Therefore to maintain a moralistic stance towards human choices, and to adjudicate that people should act only in one particular manner, biases the entire account of human purpose in a contrived direction. That is not our perspective. We need our readers to be clear about that.

The field of action is open in every direction. The choices one makes have no prescriptive definitions. In fact, any so-called "right-thinking" person may make a choice that another equally "right-thinking" person would refuse to make. Hence the standard religious judgemental stance is wrong.

Compassion is appropriate. But not judgement.

The self-righteous moralistic tone adopted by some of today's religious is a falsehood. It is generated by those who lack the courage to enter situations they need to grapple with in order to thoroughly anchor, within their own accumulated experience, knowledge of the consequences of all the types of choices that are available in the human domain.

On the other hand, those who do acquire multiplexed experience are in a position to use their resulting understanding to accurately envisage the potential outcome of any given act before they perform it.

The field of action has innumerable dimensions. It is only by randomly or systematically exploring what is available that a spiritual identity obtains the nuanced knowledge that accrues from milking human social opportunities. The lessons learned profoundly shape their understanding.

Actions produce consequences, whether comfortable or uncomfortable, mediocre, sublime, perverse or outright horrible. Having experienced them, an individual has a secure foundation on which to envisage the consequences of the choices ranged before them. When an identity's accumulated experience provides them with an extensive, multi-dimensional set of consequences, they will then be able to effortlessly and consistently select positive and loving outcomes, whatever situation they face. In the process, they will accumulate their integral Ex and advance another step in agapé.

This is the prerequisite for constructing an evolved human being. Accumulated experience brings understanding. That is all. Judgement has no place in the process. Compassion is the only appropriate attitude an evolved human being should maintain in relation to others.

Becoming an embodied human being provides a difficult path towards wisdom. It is an efficient and reliable path. But a difficult path. It comprises many false steps, wrong moves, questionable motives, and disgusting and degrading actions. But embracing them, then untangling oneself from confusing choices, is the way to acquire understanding. When that is achieved across a wide range of situations, the spiritual task is done. Other possibilities then become available that were previously inconceivable.

That is why this is not a moralistic teaching. It is a teaching full of spiritual love and compassion, of agapé and willingness to bequest agapé. Only when these qualities have become a natural inclination built into the foundations of one's spiritual identity does one enter the ranks of mature humanity. Of evolved humanity. Compassionate humanity. Humanity loving humanity. This is our perspective. Respect it.

On validly making choices

How does all this impact on the outlook of individuals living in the human domain now? If anyone wishes to comment on another's planned course of action, they could say, "You might learn something from what you're planning to do." They could say, "You'll regret that." They could say, "That will bring important understanding and wisdom." Each will be an appropriate response.

Alternatively, they could say, "I wouldn't choose that." Or, "That will be horrible!" Or, "You're a fool if you act so stupidly!" Or even, "God will bring down hellfire on you if you choose that!" None of these statements is wrong, because each in itself reflects the understanding of the person who voices it. What they say reflects their own constructed perspective.

The quality everyone making a decision needs is discernment. Discernment regarding their own personal motives, and discernment to equitably hear the spectrum of statements others make and evaluate the motives behind them. Those deciding then need the will, however strongly or poorly developed it is, to make a decision and take responsibility for it, no matter how happily or sourly it turns out. That is the correct action on every occasion, because it produces multi-layered experience.

Accumulating experience steadily progresses an individual towards wisdom. Wisdom produces freedom to move. Wisdom also strengthens will, which accelerates, or at least permits, movement from one step in agapé to the next. Objectively, achieving this step is the only goal in a life.

The transition from one step in agapé to the next normally occurs in the period between lives. It is rare for a step change to occur during an incarnation. These steps are not large. Each only produces a somewhat abrupt change in minor aspects of making choices. Moreover, the distinctions between steps are small, and there are many to be made.

This raises the popular concept of ascension. We observe that, yes, the ideal of ascension has some value, but it will happen anyway, whether one focuses on it or not. And it will only happen after the innumerable small steps in agapé have been accomplished. Besides, those who do consider ascension important have likely already adopted an intention to increase their understanding during this life. Those not concerned with ascension have many more pressing issues to attend to. As is only proper.[3]

Finally, stepping to the next level is not automatically achieved after each life. It has to be worked for. This is another argument for not "playing it safe" in one's choices. Those who are sober, upright and respectable, and don't dare anything during their life, may be judged socially superior to the individual who is whimsical, unreliable and brings a dose of misery to themselves and others. Yet it is the latter who will extract far more from their life than the former. Again, we return to discernment. Don't judge complex situations from a superficial position!

---

[3] Ascension began as a religious concept, with Jesus ascending into the heavens at the end of his time on Earth. Theosophy expanded it into the idea of ascended masters, who exist on a higher spiritual plane. From the 1960s ascension blended with the Zen notion of a satori (sudden illumination) to become an abrupt shift in spiritual levels, whether for an individual or portions of humanity. Ascension assumes moving from the physical to the spiritual is vertical. The mentors deflate this concept by suggesting movement between the spiritual and physical is lateral, not vertical. "It is possible to say, yes, there is an identity that is non-physical in nature. It makes a lateral transition to accommodate itself within a chosen species. When its experience has accumulated sufficient information, or at the demise of the member of the species concerned, it again moves laterally, at least in conceptual terms, and processes the experiences it accumulated while embodied." *The Kosmic Web*, p 139-140.

CHAPTER 9

Haric Level Perceptions

A less benevolent identity

[From Peter's journal]
Last night before going to bed I sat in meditation in the other room for a while. As has often occurred during these 20 days, I have felt visited by spiritual others. But I've not been able to see them, which has rather frustrated me. Most of them simply come, register their presence, then seem to go again.

Last night there were several, but in particular was one which came. I asked to see in that domain and got a bright light over my head, which I perceived internally. I felt this energy moving around me and encroaching on me. I then felt a curious splitting sensation in my head, as if down between the eyebrows, and got the comment, "You're a tough nut to crack, aren't you!" I didn't feel particularly like being "cracked", with the implications that involves, so sent the identity away.

For the remainder of my time here I wish to register a formal request for full clarity of vision in that domain, discussion as to why that is currently not the case, and instruction on what I can do to change this situation. I should also give thanks for the perceptiveness I do possess during this period, and the important things I have seen.

We come to you in order to respond to these statements. The opportunities we share with you, and we emphasise "share", involve observing things that are in your best interests, rather than things that may frighten you, or entertain you, or bring you pleasure. It is not part of our agenda to promote any undisciplined "cracking open". Our agenda is simply to bolster capacities which already exist in you, on those occasions, and only on those occasions, when full perception is available, and when it is in our joint best interests.

So be content with the level of perception that is innate to your current state of being. Be aware it is partial, and be alert for those varieties of identity which, as was the case last evening, do not direct benevolence towards you.

In that manner we have introduced you to another of the denizens of the spiritual domain. We intend you to become acquainted with that category of identity, so on another occasion will introduce it more fully to you.

Historical observations

We have significant material we haven't yet shared, which will round out our model. Take your attention now to the navel. In this model the seat of the soul, as it may be termed, otherwise the centre of spiritual being, is located at that position. We use the Japanese term, *hara*, to identify it.

Hara literally means belly. When the limbs are symmetrically extended, the hara is approximately at the centre of the body's mass. This is also the natural location for the centre of the spirit sphere that co-associates with the body. The sphere extends beyond the body with its limbs extended, completely enclosing it. It is a simple matter of symmetry that the centre of the body and the centre of the spirit sphere coincide. Of course, the body's centre changes when it moves. The sphere's centre does not. It continues to co-associate with the body at the hara position.

Leonardo da Vinci's Vitruvian Man effectively illustrates the model we are proposing. The kernel[1] is at the centre, but the spirit sphere extending further than is depicted in the drawing.

---

[1] The kernel is at the centre of the spirit sphere. See the note on page 51.

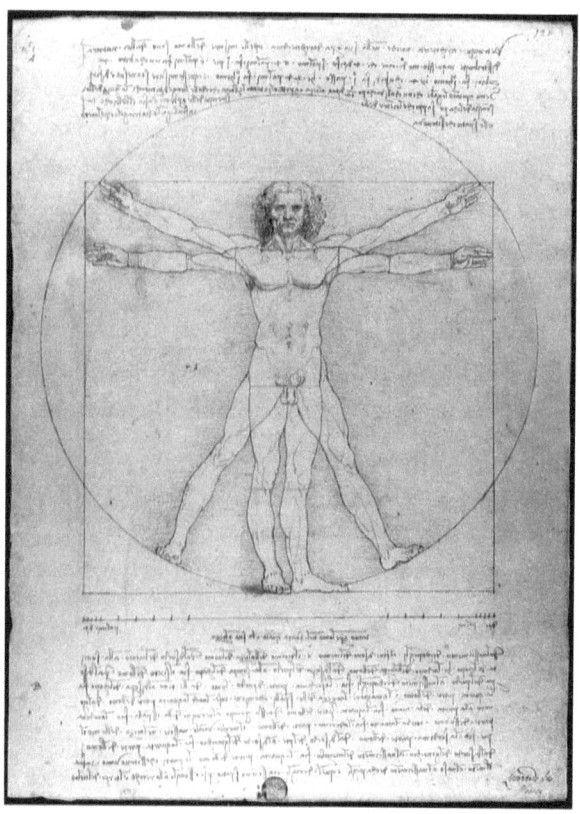

As would be expected, observer sensitivity directly impacts on what anyone perceives on any level, coarse or subtle. Several orders of magnitude of sensitivity are required to register phenomena on the hara level. To explain this, we identify three basic levels of perception. The first is the physical level, on which physical bodies are able to be perceived by human beings and other mammals. The second involves perception on the level of the aura. This is also common, but not universal. At this point we will not explain why that is so. We simply note it and observe that perception at the auric level requires greater sensitivity than perceiving physical bodies, but that it is commonly accessed, or at least the auric level is understood to be accessible. Thirdly, an even greater degree of sensitivity is required to perceive on the haric level. This explains why haric level perceptions are reported much less frequently than those on the auric level.

Haric Level Perceptions

The caduceus, carried by the Greek god Hermes, is a well-known symbol associated with the functioning of the physical form. Less commonly understood is that the caduceus directly represents the energy structure as it is perceived at the haric level. This is the level that functions at an intermediary energetic level between the spiritual identity and the physical body's aura. Knowing that you [Peter] have personally perceived the caduceus-like interior energetics of the embodied human being, we are comfortable with stating that this level exists, and that accordingly what we are saying here is not beyond the bounds of your understanding.

This is an important piece of information, because it links subtle perceptions recorded within different cultures and across time. In asserting this, we are aware that haric perception is an obscure topic, and that very few in any population are capable of accessing the haric level. And even for them it occurs infrequently. Further, scarcely any are then in a position to record their perceptions. Making a written record of this phenomenon requires an individual who has the determination to observe such things, and who also has an intellectual mindset sufficient to think about what they have perceived in terms of models and in the context of the psychology and philosophy of perception. Understandably, such individuals are rare in any population.

Nonetheless, we observe reporters exist alongside our reporter here, and that modern discussions of ancient haric perceptions are taking place

THE CADUCEUS

Depicting the ida and pingala twined around the central sushumna.

on various websites. We note there are some disagreements between older models and this one. That is because we make no mention of the higher and lower dantien.[2] They relate to perceptions from yet other levels, which we exclude from this model.

Saying this makes clear that magnitudes of perception extend beyond the hara level. However, for the sake of offering a simplified and easily grasped model for the world community, we are not going to discuss them. We do not wish to get lost in abstruse detail—and this is already quite sufficiently abstruse from almost anyone's perspective.

An authoritative caduceus interpretation

To return to the caduceus symbol, we note that the staff and the two snakes entwined around it symbolise the ida, pingala and sushumna.[3] We affirm that the depiction of this haric level perception was intended by those who originated the symbol. We further reaffirm its validity here. This is a significant point. Its existence is no longer dependent on reportage from any other time and place.

Some commentary regarding the ida, pingala and sushumna has become confused over time. Given those living who perceive at this energetic level are very few in any era, it is understandable that historically the symbols have taken on a life of their own, through repeated use, and as a result of their being reassigned from one sphere of activity to another.

But that doesn't diminish the point we are making. The caduceus, ida, pingala and shushumna are valid representations from the mythic pasts of the East and West. The pasts of both East and West are accordingly formally linked and confirmed from our level, where the truth of these matters is perceived and known. That certainty is now available to those who wish to perceive at the hara level.

To conclude, whoever sets themselves the goal of exploring this arcane

---

[2] From the Chinese, *tan tien*, energy centre.
[3] The ida, pingala and sushumna are terms from ancient Indian yoga, which identify three channels (nadi) by which energy (prana) flows from the base of the spine, through various energy centres (chakras), to the top of the head. The ida nadi is typically depicted on the left, the sushumna in the centre, and the pingala on the right.

field of perception can do so knowing that our interpretation of the caduceus and ida, pingala and shushumna is authoritative. They may also confidently make use of it when reading relevant ancient records, and the more recent commentaries on those records.

CHAPTER 10

Concluding Remarks

With those comments on the caduceus we bring this brief treatise to a close. We acknowledge this is an obscure and possibly contentious text. We also anticipate only a few will be drawn to it as they strive to understand the nature of their existence on this planet.

Nonetheless, the principles we have presented here are intended to contribute to the reshaping of humanity's conventional understanding of their identity. To repeat our main theme: Each human individual is a spiritual being. We have specified what the implications of this are for human individuals living now as embodied identities.

We add one last observation regarding this text. It is that we have discussed innate human spiritual nature without having recourse to any language evoking gods or the divine. Elsewhere we have stated that the entire human concept of the divine is a false construct.[1] We repeat that here. The concepts of gods and divinities are filled with millennia of intellectual and psychological baggage. In order to discuss the nature of human spiritual identity with sufficient clarity, detail and depth, it has been necessary to dispense with talk of the divine entirely.

This is because human assumptions regarding divinity are extensive and impossible to remove. Therefore we have not tried to do so. What has been proposed in these few pages is instead an independent and unilateral contribution to fresh discussions of being and identity. We leave it to

---

[1] *The Kosmic Web*, page 137.

readers to assimilate these concepts into their own understanding. It is each individual's responsibility to acquire wisdom, not ours.

Most sources of conventional belief concerning the nature of existence are at this point older than twenty centuries. Repeatedly throughout history individuals have proclaimed new versions of the human origin story. A small number have been accurate, given the information their authors had available to them. Like those written in other eras, this text is of its time. But we also intend it to extend beyond its time. By which we mean, we have taken what is known to the educated and extended it as far we have been able without entirely disconnecting it from current broadly agreed "reality".

Of course, some readers may think we have failed to achieve that last goal. We acknowledge that is a problem for anyone who wishes to introduce perspectives from beyond the normal human perceptual range. Thought leaders are always in the minority, by definition and in practice.

Having mapped out this particular version of the origin story, along with the terrain that led to its generation, and indicated why it will be useful to the species living on this planet—a minor species in the context of this galaxy, we might add—we bring this treatise to a end.

Our intention has been to offer a disciplined and lean set of principles that clearly identify what an individual needs to know in order to understand their purpose in living on this planet, and to appreciate, at its most fundamental level, what is involved in becoming a spiritually mature member of the human species. And, in the process, acquiring wisdom.

The extent to which this perspective on the origins and endpoint of the human population is widely accepted is irrelevant. Many competing narratives have been conceived throughout history, each with their subtle variations. However, the broad outline is sufficiently established for this reincarnational perspective to be generally recognisable as true. To conclude:

A human is a spiritual identity first, foremost and always.

It periodically incarnates, then returns to where it came from.

It does so for its own reasons.

It achieves maturity by collecting information.

Its eventual destiny is beyond description.

All that may be confirmed is that the entire sequence of developing independent identity is matched by its return to the state of complete dissolution in larger understanding.

We end by offering love and good will to all those, embodied or not, who seek wisdom.

Appendices

APPENDIX 1

Definitions and Co-ordinate Descriptions

Definitions

- *Spiritual domain* = the realm of continuous existence of the human spirit and others
- *Astral domain* = one of the lower regions of the spiritual domain
- *Lower astral* = subset of the astral domain where humans exist while embodied. Identified by grey light giving somewhat obscured vision in a vast space commonly known as the Void.
- *Higher astral* = subset of the astral domain identified by clear light giving unobscured vision in a vast space.

A coordinate system in the Void

Human beings occupy the lower astral domain, part of the extended domain of spiritual space. It is possible to identify an individual's location in that domain. Because the location is in the Void, which is part of spiritual space and not physical space, the location is described in terms of frequency co-ordinates, not spatial co-ordinates. The mentors have proposed the concept of agapéic space to identify an individual human being's location in the Void. Location in agapéic space is specified using three axes:
- Agapé, hierarchy and willingness to bequest agapé.
- Each of these three axes has a range of values. An individual's location is identified by evaluating how much they manifest agapé, hierarchy and willingness to bequest agapé.
- As an individual increases any of their agapé, hierarchy and willingness to bequest agapé they change location in agapéic space.
- A field gradient, which measures the change of location in agapéic space, may be plotted as an arc through agapéic space.

- An individual's attributes of intrinsic energy value, will magnitude, and movement freedom magnitude, dictate their change in location. An individual achieves freedom of movement in the astral domain through the sum of their embodied acts intended by love, accumulated over all embodied lifetimes.

Detailing the three axes

Fundamental dimensions of this spiritual domain model:

Dimension 1 label	= agapé (a)
Dimension 2 label	= hierarchy (h)
Dimension 3 label	= willingness to bequest agapé (wtba)
Agapé value range	= 25,000 to 35,000 agape frequency units (afu)
Hierarchy value range	= 0 to 100
Willingness value range	= 41,000 to 45,000 wtba units
Agapé divisions	= unitary steps in agapéic frequency
Hierarchy divisions	= unitary percentage steps (1%)
Willingness division	= unitary steps in wtba and their subdivisions

Relations

- The basic volume of existence = a x h x wtba = agapéic space.
- Lower astral plane (a subset of agapéic space) = h x wtba = a plane within which a position is determined for each identity.

Fields

- The positioning field is $Es = h \times a^2$. This is a curvilinear field of vertically centralising tendency having thickness within, and being coextensive with, the a x wtba plane.
- The migration field is $Ex = \int Ex$. This is a hara-level incremental shift generated by actions intended by love. Many actions must be integrated to create a one-step migration or incremental shift in agapé.

APPENDIX 2

The Transmission of Wisdom: The Task of Gnostic Intermediaries[1]

by Roger Walsh, M.D., Ph.D.
Dept of Psychiatry and Human Behavior, University of California

> Happy are those who find wisdom ...
> She is more precious than jewels,
> and nothing you desire can compare with her ...
> Her ways are ways of pleasantness,
> and all her paths are peace ...
> Get insight, get wisdom: do not forget.
> (Jewish Torah, *Proverbs* 3:13, 17, 4:5)

A central claim of contemplative disciplines is that they cultivate wisdom. In fact, cultivating wisdom is one of the seven central practices common to the world's great religious and spiritual traditions (Walsh, 1999).

Likewise, a central claim of many contemplative psychologies, philosophies, and texts is that parts of them conceptualize and analyze aspects of this wisdom. Examples include psychologies such as Buddhist Abhidharma, philosophies such as Chinese Taoism or Indian Vedanta, and texts such as the Christian contemplative *Philokalia*.

What we usually think of as wisdom, I would define as deep understanding of, and practical skill in responding to, the central existential issues of life. Greek philosophers referred to this understanding as *sophia*, and to this practical skill as *phronesis* (Sternberg & Jordan, 2005).

However, the wisdom that contemplative disciplines claim to cultivate, and that these philosophies and psychologies analyze, adds some-

---

[1] Originally published in *Journal of Transpersonal Research*, 2009, Vol. 1, pp 114-117.

thing further. For contemplative wisdom finds its deepest basis in a direct, intuitive transcendental apprehension (Walsh, 1999; Wilber, 2006). This wisdom has many names, such as *gnosis* (Christianity), *jnana* (Hinduism), *prajna* (Buddhism), *hokhmah* (Judaism), and *ma'rifah* (Islam). This transrational wisdom, which we might call *transnoia*, seems to foster *sophia* and *phronesis*, while also adding further depth and richness to them. It is therefore not surprising that some of history's greatest contemplatives have also been regarded as some of history's wisest sages, e.g. Christianity's Dionysus, Hinduism's Shankara, Islam's Ibn Arabi, Kashmir Shaivism's Abinavagupta, Neo-Confucianism's Wang Yang-ming, and the Buddha.

However, the distinctive nature of contemplative wisdom immediately presents a challenge to anyone who would comprehend it, and even more to anyone who would communicate it. For this wisdom is largely obtained in altered states of consciousness and postconventional stages of development that are usually accessible only after considerable contemplative practice. Understanding contemplative wisdom may therefore require experiencing these states, stages, and relevant insights, for oneself.

This is a specific example of a more general principle that there are limitations on understanding transpersonal experiences and insights without direct experience of them. These limitations can be understood in several ways. For example, they can be considered in terms of states of consciousness as examples of state-specific knowledge (Tart, 2001). Likewise, they can be considered developmentally as stage-specific understanding; in classical epistemological terms as the requirement that we open "the eye of contemplation" (Wilber, 1996); and linguistically as the inherent difficulty of understanding a signifier (word or term) without having experienced the relevant signified experience (Wilber, 2001).

What then does it require to apprehend and understand the transpersonal wisdom of contemplative disciplines? In a word, it requires practice. One must take up a contemplative practice so as to open one's own "eye of contemplation." Only by actually doing contemplative practices can we mature and open ourselves to the deeper insights and understandings they offer. As the translator of Patanjali's yoga sutras wrote:

It is axiomatic in the yoga tradition that "knowledge is different in different states of consciousness" (Rig Veda). In other words our level of consciousness completely determines how much of the truth we see in any given situation. The clearer our minds, the more correctly we evaluate our experience (Shearer, 1989, p. 26).

However, to communicate these insights and understandings effectively requires something more. It requires that we become *gnostic intermediaries*. So what is a gnostic intermediary? Carl Jung (Jung, 1966) used the term to refer to Wilhelm, the translator of the *I Ching*, who Jung suggested was able to transmit, not only the ideas, but also the underlying wisdom of the *I Ching*. Jung does not seem to have developed the concept further, but we can amplify it as follows.

First, let me suggest a definition. "A *gnostic intermediary* is a person who is able to effectively translate and transmit contemplative wisdom from one culture or community to another. This translation/transmission can be across cultures (e.g. Indian yogic wisdom to Western culture) or across times (from archaic language and concepts into contemporary forms, e.g. communicating early Christian contemplative wisdom to contemporary Christian communities)."

What does this require? Well, it seems to require three tasks and three corresponding capacities:

> First, one must imbibe and become the wisdom oneself, since while one can *have* knowledge, one must *be* wise. This, of course, is a major task. In fact, when we are talking about profound contemplative wisdom it can take a lifetime. The essence of this step is contemplative practice.
>
> The second requirement for gnostic intermediaries is linguistic and conceptual competence. They must master the language and conceptual system of the people and culture to which they wish to communicate. For professionals, this means mastering one's professional conceptual frame work, e.g., psychology or philosophy.
>
> The third requirement is translational. Gnostic intermediar-

ies must be able to translate the wisdom from the wisdom bearing culture or tradition into the language and conceptual system of the recipient community. The goal is to make the wisdom understandable, legitimate, and even compelling.

This is the challenge and opportunity for all those who would draw from and communicate the world's contemplative wisdom. As such it is a challenge and opportunity of our time for teachers of contemplation, for transpersonal and integral psychologists, and for scholars of the world's contemplatively based psychologies and philosophies.

It is a large task. However, it is also an essential one for our time, as scholars and practitioners seek to understand the deeper significance of contemplative practices, psychologies, and philosophies. It may also be vitally important for our culture and species, which are drowning in information, but comparatively lacking in wisdom. In fact, it may be that we are in a race between wisdom and world disaster, between consciousness and catastrophe. We are in great need of wisdom, and of gnostic intermediaries to communicate it.

References

Jung, C. G. (1966). *Spirit in Man, Art and Literature. Collected Works of C.G. Jung, Vol. 15*. Princeton, NJ: Princeton University Press.

Shearer, P. (Trans.). (1989). *Effortless Being: The yoga sutras of Patanjali*. London: Unwin.

Sternberg, R. & J. Jordan. (2005). *A Handbook of Wisdom*. NY: Cambridge University Press.

Tart, Ch. (2001). *States of Consciousness*. NY: Dutton.

Walsh, R. (1999). *Essential Spirituality: The seven central practices*. NY: Wiley & Sons.

Wilber, K. (2001). *A Theory of Everything: An integral vision for business, politics, science and spirituality*. Boston: Shambhala.

Wilber, K. (1996). *A Brief History of Everything*. Boston: Shambhala.

APPENDIX 3

The Universe is in a Multiverse

Excerpted from *The Kosmic Web*
by Peter Calvert and Keith Hill[1]

The origin of the universe is well known to human scientists in a purely physical sense. The emergence of a singularity and the big bang that followed is an adequate explanation for what happened to bring this universe into existence. What is not well known is the spiritual intent behind that coming to be.

What we will attempt to describe is something of that intent and how it has created what is—for creation there certainly was. However, creation did not occur in the way that is traditionally and religiously understood. We will come back to the issue of creation presently. For now we need to clarify the nature and purpose of *this* universe, it being the universe humanity lives in and perceives.

The universe is in a multiverse

First what is required is the adoption of a field view. That is, you must picture an extensive field within which not just this universe but multiple universes are expanding and contracting. Science has called this the multiverse model. We affirm that this model is valid, although not in the way cosmologists currently speculate. As we will show, while both the religious and the scientific descriptions of the origin of the universe are valid in part, neither is a wholly successful description. There is much that both perspectives leave out.

---

[1] The text here is channelled. From *The Kosmic Web* (2015), Attar Books, pp 33-39.

How many universes are there within the multiverse? The number is only of theoretical concern to human beings, given no physical observation can possibly be made of another universe from this universe to validate what we might state. Nonetheless, we affirm there are a handful of universes currently going through their cycles of expansion and contraction, between five and ten in number. We will not be more precise for a reason we will shortly come to.

Each universe has specific parameters within which it exists. Just as scientists have identified certain numerical values in relation to this universe, such as the strength of gravity and the values of the weak and strong forces, and they know that these values are basic to this universe being what it is, so the parameter values basic to other universes are different, and consequently give rise to a different universal nature and conditions for existence.

Accordingly, it can be seen that the universe humanity exists within is actually part of a multiple initiative. It is not a sole attempt to conjure something from nothing, as the philosophers say. It is part of a wider experiment to explore many varied possibilities of existence. And we say *experiment* advisedly, because this is certainly one way the multiverse may be viewed. In fact, the model of the multiverse as an experiment is the model we prefer for this kosmic meta-explanation.

The multiverse is an experiment

In order to convey something of the nature of the multiverse, we projected an image of the multiverse into the mind of Peter Calvert. This indicates all the universes are connected within the field to an intent named the *observer*.

The *observer* is that which initiated the multiverse experiment. The *observer* selected the experimental parameters for each universe, then set them in motion. Given each universe is at a different phase within its complete repeated cycles of expansions and contractions, some will cease to be before others. They will, or will not, be replaced by other universes according to the *observer's* intent. So this initiative of the multiverse is an ongoing process, the scale of which is beyond the understanding of any physical mind.

PETER'S VISION OF THE MULTIVERSE

In this sketch, the uniform background is the featureless unmanifest and the spheres are the manifest multiple universes asynchronously and repeatedly expanding and contracting at their individual rate. That rate was approximately 1 to 3 seconds. Each universe manifested a similar maximum diameter before collapsing again. The web represents the tethering process of sustained intention to the *observer* in this experiment in the field of existence.

The implication is that in the same way that one would locate significant numbers of firecrackers somewhat distant from a house for simple reasons of safety, so also in that field of observation the undetermined behaviour of the universes would be placed at some distance from the *observer* for safety in the experimental setup.

Space seemed unlimited above, below and all around, being everywhere uniform in character. The *observer* was not observed by me but was known to be there. The individual universes seemed somehow tethered to the edge of the viewing field, equidistant in a radial arc from the locus of perception by the *observer*. I sensed my view was partial, but have no way of knowing what lay beyond the limits of my perception, although there were no other features visible in that scene.

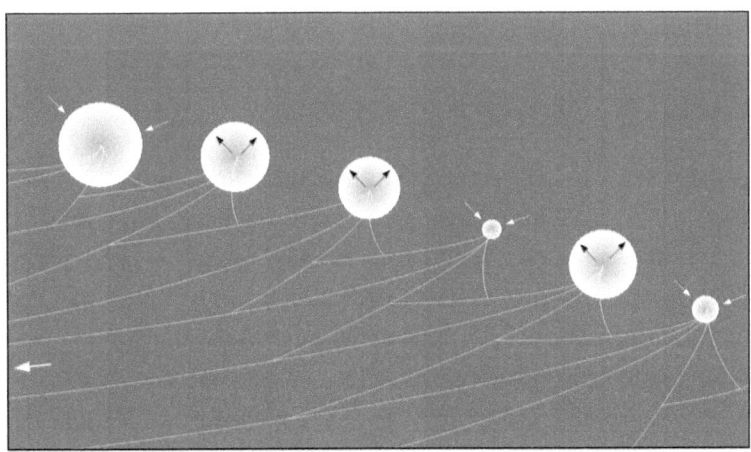

This explains why we cannot assign a particular number to the universes within the multiverse. The human time scale is simply too truncated to accommodate the vastness of what is occurring. Humanity lives in a *now* that simply does not exist for us. Or for the multiverse. Or the *observer*. We exist outside the spacetime continuum humanity lives within. For us to generate a sample, which is what we would need to do, by making a theoretical slice through spacetime and then use that as a reference moment to definitively state, "As of now x number of universes exist within the multiverse," is ultimately an arbitrary exercise. There is no now. There is a range of current existence. From which we can derive an approximation only. Which we have done.

Of course, underpinning this entire kosmic construct is an assumption that the *observer* possesses the knowledge necessary to preselect values that result in a stable universe, which consequently functions according to the preset parameters, and does so in a manner that is consistent with the intent that brought it into existence. So this is not a randomised initiative. An infinity of universes has not been brought into existence out of a vague hope that one universe out of millions might succeed. This is definitely not the case. It is an intelligently intended and constructed experiment.

In this sense, the universe may be said to be created. Deliberately so. But we are not talking about some all-powerful God controlling all existence in the way religions conceive. We have no intention to do that. To expand on this we will discuss first the purpose of the experiment, then the nature of creation.

The *observer's* experimental purpose

Many scientists attempt to deny that there is any purpose to the universe and what exists in it, that everything happens accidentally, entirely as a matter of chance. They adopt this view because the only coherent alternative view is the traditional religious view, which is that God created everything. This could be a straightforward notion, but theologians have added to the idea of God as creator by also claiming that God is controller.

This notion of God as controller is difficult to sustain, because when anyone with an unbiased mind examines the universe they perceive that everything is not controlled, that chance and chaos are built into the universe's very fabric. So it is valid that the scientifically inclined reject the notion of God as controller. However, because the religious have tied the idea of God as creator to that of controller, the scientific happily jettison the notion of the creator God too.

This is an example of the confusion human beings generate when they over-speculate. Neither religious metaphysics nor scientific naturalism are accurate. As a corrective to partial thinking we present the notion that the intent of the *observer* certainly led to the multiverse coming into existence in what could be said, using somewhat limited human terminology, to be a creative act. But no ultimate control is subsequently exerted in the traditional religious sense.

The *observer* has never been involved in any physical universe. Nor will it ever be. After setting the underlying parameter values for each universe, the *observer* has stood back, to use another inadequate human metaphor, and observes what occurs. This is somewhat like the Deist notion that a personal God created the world then stood back and let creation function according to natural laws. Yet the analogy works only partially. The *observer* is nothing like a personal God or a person of any kind. Instead, the personal functions at the level of nodes of Dao-consciousness.

To come back to the origin of this universe, and to use current scientific terminology, following the big bang the laws of physics spontaneously transformed energy into matter, matter developed into gas clouds, gravitational forces drew the gas into stars and planets, and on certain of these planets environmental niches formed, some of which were supportive of life, in which life eventually emerged.

It could be said that behind the creation of each universe is a multiplexed intent to generate environments in which physical life, and ever more varied and complex forms of physical life, comes into existence and evolves. But throughout this extensive process there is never any intent, at the *observer's* level, to control either the process or the outcome. From the *observer's* perspective there is also no attachment to what happens to any single life form.

So the multiverse is an extended experiment of inconceivable magnitude in which sets of opportunities have been constructed for the purpose of facilitating the emergence of ever more varied life forms. There is benign goodwill at the outcome of each universe. But no outcome is predetermined.

The *observer* is part of the Dao

Accordingly, it can be affirmed that there is a spiritual level initiative to generate all the many domains of the physical. The spiritual existed before the physical. The physical is a sub-formation, a subconstuct, of a profound intent. The *observer* is the active manifestation of that intent. But behind the *observer* is an even deeper existent. We call this the Dao. We define the Dao as the ultimate unmanifest. The *observer* is the active force, for want of a better term, within the ultimate unmanifest. It too is unmanifest, of course. Simply, the Dao is the ultimate source of all that is and the *observer* is its intent.

We are trying to explain matters that exist at the edge, in fact beyond the edge, of human comprehension. Words are needed to explain anything. We have chosen the words Dao and *observer* because they are relatively neutral terms, at least in the context of secular Western English language.

There is a natural tendency among human beings to be either overly respectful of traditional terminology or overly disrespectful. Neither approach is helpful. Many religious terms were invented in an attempt to explain arcane matters. Over time they inevitably accrued layers of theological dust, and their original intent became tarnished, then completely obscured. Many years later others have come along and rejected those traditional terms completely. Yet underneath the dust, under all the speculative and self-aggrandising verbiage, there remains a kernel of truth. We are trying to extract that kernel, polish it, and represent it from a fresh perspective using new terminology.

So if the term Dao, which is taken from the Chinese, or the term *observer*, which has connotations of the laboratory experimenter, conjure for some readers traditional concepts of God, we cannot stop them thinking in that way. However, we are deliberately attempting to avoid referencing religious God language. Aspects of what we are saying here have certainly been described before, in other cultures and eras, in religious contexts. We are merely developing and updating those older concepts, constructing culturally relevant models and using terminology appropriate to these times.

Accordingly, whenever we use the term Dao, we ask you to think of the ultimate, inexplicable unmanifest. And when we use the term *observer* keep in mind that you, with every sentient being, are also an observer. The creative initiative the *observer* undertook that led to the coming into existence of this universe, which ultimately generated the experiences that are your life, also exists in you. You can undertake creative initiatives and generate circumstances beneficial to yourself and others. You can set up experiments. You can bring into existence what previously did not exist—all in a far more limited way than the *observer* does, of course. But the *observer's* intent is not alien from yours. It is the same. Your desire to live a fruitful life is completely aligned to the *observer's* fecund intent to generate what has ultimately given you that opportunity.

We repeat, all this is an attempt to subvert the traditional view of God and the spiritual as separate and wholly distinct from physical human existence. This is quite incorrect. As we keep repeating, and as we intend to show through the remainder of this text, the spiritual and the physical are utterly and irrevocably intertwined. This starts with all physical universes being an extension of the intent of the spiritual.

APPENDIX 4

A Confused Climber

This is the record of a soul rescue, in which a deceased man was helped to understand he had died and needed to move on from his current transitional state. Three meditators were present: Peter Calvert, Richard Bentley and Janet Oliver. The voice of the deceased man speaks through Peter and is italicised.

P   There's something strange in my neck area, I don't understand it, as if someone has been hung or had their neck broken, either deliberately killed or in a fall, I don't know which. And maybe a belief that speech is thereby not possible. I'm not sure of any of that.

> The mentors [through Peter]:
> We begin a brief illustration of the way in which symptoms can be interpreted non-verbally. The neck in question was broken by accidental fall. The owner of the neck is present, yet declines to speak due to a persistent belief that it is a controlling factor for them, even without a body. This recalcitrant individual has for many years refused to acknowledge the reality of their demise on the one hand, even though they react as if the demise were true on the other hand. This inner conflict has locked them into an inability to proceed further. Will you help this one?

R   We will try. [Addressing the deceased.] Can you convey your message and thoughts to us by projecting them into the mind of Peter, who will speak for you. We wish to know what you have to say.

---

[1] From a channelled session, 18 September 2008.

A Confused Climber

X   I seem to be confused, because I know my neck is severely damaged. I know that I wasn't able to speak for some time. And then ... a kind of darkness came ... and that hasn't changed. I thought I couldn't talk. I thought I couldn't move. I didn't seem able to move. And I couldn't see. I couldn't see myself. I thought I was blind. I tried to call out, yet there seemed to be nobody responding. It was very confusing! I grew despairing. I felt no one near, heard nothing. I was confused! Where had they gone? Surely they would come to get me? But no one came, and I lost track of time. And it feels like a long time, or it could be yesterday, I can't tell the difference. It was very confusing for me.

R   You are communicating well with us. What would you like to happen now? What's your wish?

X   Clarify my understanding! I don't know my circumstances. Where am I? Where am I? I don't know where I am. I was climbing, and climbing well and quickly, and proceeding according to plan. It was a good face to climb! And there was my companion, I thought. But I can't find any trace of him now.

R   It appears you may have fallen and broken, and you're now in a transition stage. You spoke before of people not coming. Who would you like to come for you?

X   I can't accept what you say! There is no reality to it. Surely I'm lying on the ground somewhere, and someone will come. I couldn't have fallen far. I was roped to my companion. How can this be? I seem to see myself swinging like on a safety rope. But I can't feel it. I can't ... I hear nothing. Surely there should be sounds?

R   You're swinging from a safety rope. What happens next?

X   The procedure is that the other pulls one up to safety. That's the whole point of it. Unless they fell too? Or let me go? Or the rope broke or was cut?

R   Have you called for the other?

X   I thought so. I heard no reply. I didn't understand. There ought to be somebody above me supporting me so when I fell I remained safe. Where has he gone? Or is it ... I who have gone? But where? This is ...? There should be a logical picture applicable here, there should be a reason! Something can't just stop!

R   Cast your awareness around. What do you perceive?

X   *I perceive nothing. I'm isolated. I've felt nothing, heard nothing, seen nothing!*

R   Look for light.

X   *Why? What good would that do?*

R   There may be something you're not looking for therefore you don't see it. Perhaps it would be helpful.

X   *There's no logic in that as an action!*

R   Nevertheless it may be worth trying.

X   *I can't even see my hand, let alone anything else! I don't seem to have any eyes that work anymore. I must have fallen into a cave, or ... it's just so strange!*

R   How have you perceived us?

X   *I don't know. There just seemed to be a presence. I seemed to hear a voice for the first time in a very long time. I won't go until I know where I'm going. Otherwise I cling here. My life depends on it! Who knows where I would go if I let go? In the mountains you have to learn how to hang on! To be prepared to do so long past your beliefs about your endurance have been surpassed. Your life depends upon it. Sometimes your companion's life depends upon it. You undertake to do these things! In good faith, I can't stop doing that. It's too important. I must stay where I am.*

R   You seek an explanation for where you are and why you are there and what is happening. Who is the one person you would trust to provide you with the right answer?

X   *My father. He knows these things better than I. But I last saw him a long time ago. I don't know where he is.*

R   Perhaps you could call for him? Ask him to come.

X   *But how could he know where to find me? That's not possible. Even I don't know where I am! How can he find me if I can't tell him where to come to? There is no logic in that.*

R   Perhaps his perception is different from yours and he will know where to find you. If you don't call, how will he know?

X   *How do I know where to go? How can I move from here? I can't find my hands!*

R   Cast your mind and your thoughts out to your father.

X   *He is here. He's trying to talk to me and I don't understand him. He can't have come from nowhere. I don't understand, it's completely bizarre! He seems to want me to go with him.*

R   Then go with him. He's the person that you trust.

X   *He's in fog. Strange black fog! I can see again! And it's not where I was. I will go. I will go with him. He has found me!*

R   Go well.

P   It was odd, because one seemed to be towing the other. That reluctant idiot being towed away out of the darkness into a much lighter place, not fully light, but ... That was weird. An interesting self-immobilising knot of beliefs. Recalcitrant is probably an applicable word.

APPENDIX 5

A Mischievous Spirit

This is the record of a soul rescue, involving a deceased young man. Two meditators were present: Peter Calvert and Richard Bentley. The voice of the deceased man speaks through Richard and is italicised.

> [The mentors [through Peter]:
> There has been an opportunity for you both to settle. The opportunity can now be broadened to those any or many who may benefit by your tender ministrations. We bring one with whom you may care to interact.

R We welcome you. How may we help you?

P I'd be happy to talk for anybody if I could sense any presence, but I don't. Do you?

R I think I did initially, as you were speaking. I thought, "Oh, there's somebody trying to take me over, or something!" It was a funny woozy feeling.

P Would you be willing to talk for them?

R Yes. But I don't feel any presence.

P Nevertheless, if the contact has been established with you. It certainly wasn't with me. Then I would say, "Welcome, and how may we help?" See if you can allow some interaction.

R Mm.

P Please communicate with us through Richard to express your concerns, or to pass comment or even judgement or in any other way communicate with us. ... Do you pick up anything low on the right-hand side? That's where my attention seems to have been taken.

---

[1] From a channelled session, 18 September 2008.

R   No. I'm not sure if I'm getting something or not. I'll verbalise it and see.

P   Good.

X   (In an altered voice) *I see you two for what you are! I'm much wiser than you.*

P   (Already concluding from sensing this entity's energetic signature that we had a mischievous spirit with us, and therefore saying in mock seriousness:) I'm delighted to hear it! Please share with us?

X   *You sitting there expecting to talk to spirits, spooks. It's very funny!*

P   Why is that?

X   *It is so pathetic.*

P   Ah. Do you have a better plan?

X   *Oh, I have a much better plan.*

P   What's that?

X   *I'll go back into my cave, and you'll see.*

P   What will we see?

X   *That would be telling.*

P   And how may we address you?

X   *You can call me "Sir".*

P   Welcome, Sir.

X   *Sir Thomas of Stepford.*

P   Sir Thomas of Stepford!

X   *That's a silly name I made up.*

P   Ok. Do you have another one?

X   *I may have done. I don't remember. It doesn't matter.*

P   Ok. Well, just for fun, until you come up with a better one, can I call you Sir? Or would you prefer Thomas?

X   *Sir Thomas will be just fine.*

P   Now, Sir Thomas, when were you alive last?

X   *1642.*

P   1642!

X   *Columbus sailed the ocean blue.*

P   Ahh, so you got taught that at school, too!

X   *Yes.*

P   And where and when did you learn that?

X   *I don't remember. Maybe it was 1868, or something. Or maybe 1928. I don't remember, and it doesn't matter.*
P   Mm. And what was the last country you lived in?
X   *England.*
P   So you are English. And when you lived in England, how did you get about?
X   *Hopped and skipped and jumped. There were horses.*
P   How old are you?
X   *I don't know.*
P   How big were you when you last remember?
X   *Maybe I was about 18. I don't remember.*
P   If you think about now, what year do you think this might be?
X   *Mm, 1948 come to mind.*
P   1948. Okay. It's quite a lot past that now, because this is 2010.
X   *Oh! Think of all the dinners I've missed!*
P   Indeed! What a lot of good food you've missed! So if 1948 is the last date you remember, you've been dead for nearly 60 years.
X   *Oh, no wonder I don't smell too good.*
P   (Laughs) It could be so.
X   *You're more fun than I thought.*
P   Glad to entertain you. What have you been doing during all that time?
X   *Oh, wandering about, creating mischief. Talking to people like you who try to contact the other side but don't really know what you are looking for. So I come up and gently prod and prompt ...*
P   Yes, make a little contribution.
X   *I like to think of it as fun and teasing.*
P   How have you been responded to?
X   *Oh, I've got a lot of old ladies and all sorts of people. They're really enthusiastic and I tell them all sorts of rubbish that I make up.*
P   (laughs) I bet you do! Is that fun for you?
X   *Oh yes! I think they are so stupid!*
P   Well done! And is that something you want to continue with?
X   *Well, I don't see why not. There doesn't seem to be anything else.*
P   Oh, really! Hasn't become just a bit boring?

X   Well, not ... not exactly boring. But I have to think of new things to do and say and ...
P   So it's become a little bit tedious, eh?
X   I guess so.
P   Is there something else you'd like to do?
X   Sky diving would be good. Just joking.
P   (laughs) I guess you'd find that quite easy at the moment anyway.
X   Yes, it's not ... I'm just there, where I want to be, or I just think, and ... I miss the physical sensation.
P   Tell me about that.
X   Not able to feel my body, and so I can't go for a swim, or whatever.
P   Yep. What were your favourite activities?
X   Swimming and sex. But we didn't do much swimming.
P   It might have been a bit cold.
X   Yes.
P   Okay. When you look around yourself, what do you see?
X   It's like a vast room. But then it has rocks and landscape in it.
P   Is it light or dark?
X   It's in-between.
P   Has anybody ever told you what to expect when you get to this kind of state?
X   No.
P   Did you go to school?
X   No. Maybe for a short time.
P   Did you ever go to church?
X   Yes. It was awful.
P   Really? Tell me about that.
X   The priests would round us up and herd us in and hit us, and then tell us we were wicked and sinful and make us feel guilty. But I didn't take much notice after a while. It was easier to do what we were told.
P   Of course. Were you under their protection? Or confined with them? Or ...
X   Yes, I think it must have been a school or orphanage or something like that. So I went back and I haunted the priest, ha ha. I made him very uncomfortable!

P (Laughs) Was that satisfying?

X *Oh yes! Oh yes, I did that for some time.*

P If you enjoyed that so much did you do that with anybody else?

X *A few other priests and clergymen and people I didn't like. And then other people didn't seem to be around ... Then there were these people trying to make contact with the spirit world, and they were much more fun!*

P Were they spiritualists in England?

X *I think so.*

P Didn't they suggest something about your condition and somewhere else for you to be?

X *Some did, but I just ignored them and went and found the ones I could play with.*

P Okay. Do you have any interest in exploring those possibilities now?

X *Exploring what possibilities?*

P Well, of thinking there may be somewhere else to be and things to do that might be more interesting and enjoyable, and maybe even challenging and something that you could not only have fun with but also learn from?

X *Oh yes. What do you suggest?*

P What I suggest is that kind of place is a very loving place. A place full of light and freedom and possibility. Not at all boring!

X *I would like that. I've had no love.*

P Yes. If there were to be somebody that you remembered with affection, who might that be who could take you to a place like that?

X *My mother.*

P What was her name?

X *I'm not sure. Doris comes to mind, but I'm not sure. She died.*

P How old were you when she died?

X *Two.*

P Two. Just a wee thing. She's probably very willing to come to you if you were to ask for her.

X *Where is she?*

P What I suggest you do is just look up and all around and feel your memory of her and the kind of feeling that you would have felt with her before she died. Just the kind of really comfortable, loving, protective kind of warm gentle feeling ...

R (Starts) I think he's gone.

P Very good.

R Oohh! That was a (indistinct). Half the time it felt like it was me, and I really wasn't sure, but when you asked if there was somebody, or you mentioned it was a loving place, that was a trigger. I don't know what to make of that.

P An individual of those qualities certainly would have come up from some distance down. It's consistent with the perception that my whole attention was taken quite a long way down, quite close in front and a little bit to the right. I've met one or two from those levels, and they manifest those sort of qualities. Sir who? (Laughs) Well, that was fun. He had a manner about him, didn't he.

R Yes, sort of cynical initially, but goading.

P But I didn't feel any sense of real evil. Just mischievous, really.

R Yes.

P Wanting to play and be provocative. Poke borax.

R Mm. Scared the shit out of little old ladies!

P Or beguile them, perhaps.

R Mm.

P Okay, I'd like to take the opportunity to give thanks for that opportunity to be of assistance to somebody who clearly needed some! and to affirm the relevance of that kind of service.

APPENDIX 5

The Plane of Morality

This is transcribed from a meditation session involving Peter and Janet. When Janet was receiving a message from the mentors the recorder's batteries went flat, so the message was recorded 10 minutes later, with Janet repeating the material from memory.

The material consists of spiritual advice about using a tool to give oneself clarity about which direction to take when confronted with a choice or temptation.

J   They [the mentors] spoke of the model which Peter has been developing, which consists of a sphere of intersecting planes. These planes represent the variables which create any situation an individual may find themselves in. Because of the complexity of visualising such a system in perpetual motion, it's suggested it is possible to pause the model and thus establish two intersecting axes. The upper right-hand quadrant represents the most positive situations, and in the extreme upper right-hand corner stands the individual to whom we would aspire to be closest to. This individual emulates all the good qualities that a person could manifest in any particular situation. While we may never reach the full potential of this individual, we may aspire to any particular point on that plane that we feel we could achieve.

The lower left-hand quadrant represents the region of darkness, where the negative aspects of any situation or behaviour are manifest. When confronted with a challenge or temptation, one would place oneself in a position in the upper left-hand quadrant, if in a situation of temptation where no negative deed has yet been performed, yet negative thoughts have become manifest. From here one can see the direction in which one

---

[1] From a meditation session, 25 February 2006.

could move when freewill is exercised. So this particular tool acts as a road map. By actually positioning yourself on this plane you can perceive with clarity where you are at, and where you want to go.

What I can see now is that the lower right-hand quadrant is where you would position yourself if you had already taken negative action, but had positive desires to reverse the situation.

P   So the axes then become an intention vs action pair, with constructive/destructive values superimposed on it?

J   Yes, that's true.

P   It's clearer than before.

J   Okay, that's good.

P   And the example was …

J   The example was, if you were in a situation where you were tempted to pilfer or embezzle funds from a company you worked for. If you hadn't performed the deed, you would position yourself in the upper left-hand quadrant. If you chose to resist the temptation you would be positioning yourself in the right-hand quadrant, in the light, but perhaps at a distance from the ultimate being. Whereas you could choose to carry out the deed and descend into the darkness. Or you could choose to stay where you are.

P   I was going to say that I had been mentally addressing the question before you started talking during our meditation. Something about how you can map actions and consequences in a more explicit way than the very fuzzy way that I certainly often do. This seems to be a response to that inner question. That's really good!

To the reader

Attar Books appreciates our readers' support. We request you consider posting an online review where you bought this book.

The following five books are referenced in the introduction and text. They offer further details on concepts introduced here, and related ideas.

LEARNING WHO YOU ARE

Learning Who You Are offers a contemporary take on the age-old questions of who we are and why we are here. The book builds on current scientific knowledge to show how the physical and spiritual realms are interlinked. It does this by presenting a number of innovative models and conceptual frameworks that mesh with twenty-first century understanding. The book also discusses the process of validating these models and concepts empirically, through observation, and explains how meditation may be used to expand vision within and beyond the everyday self. Throughout, the emphasis is on practical processes, focused on the here and now, yet which have the potential to open a doorway into the beyond.

All this is explored using an open-ended, experimental approach that challenges the rigid dichotomies of the past, such as the mundane many vs the enlightened few, and the profane human vs the sacred divine. Historically, the notion of divinity has erected a barrier between humanity and the spiritual realm, which signals that whatever happens in the spiritual dimension is distant and so must remain an unfathomable mystery. *Learning Who You Are* alternatively, and controversially, asserts that the spiritual domain is not divine; individual human spirits, enlightened or otherwise, are not special; and the spiritual is neither distant nor unfathomable.

The absence of divinity means no Divine Being is pushing or pulling any of us during the course of our lives. So understanding the fundamental nature of our existence doesn't depend on divine decree or sacred revelation. We are already spiritual, hence appreciating the spiritual bases of our existence may be achieved straightforwardly—should we wish to do so, and be willing to make the effort required to discern them.

Learning Who You Are offers the spiritually inquisitive and adventurous a unique, contemporary perspective on what it is to be human, and what may be achieved while living on this often perplexing planet.

THE KOSMIC WEB

The Kosmic Web offers fuller explanations of many concepts presented in introductory form in this book. It begins at the beginning, with the creation of the multiverse, then discusses the seeding of ecosystems, biological life and humanity. It goes on to explore many of the concepts introduced in these pages, but in much greater detail, specifically: the nature of Dao, the nature of the electrospiritual, the function of the aura, and the evolution of nodes and node fragments. It concludes with a consideration of the traditional Great Chain of Being, which is updated into the concept of the web of life. *The Kosmic Web* is recommended as the primary text for appreciating the guides' view of existence.

"The nature of the body, including its basic shape and functioning, is well known. What is not well known is the nature and shape of the spiritual identity that locates itself beside, within and through the body. The individual spiritual identity, and we are talking now in an energetic sense, exists in the shape of a sphere. Its structure is globular. Imagine a ball, say a soccer ball, with the hexagons and pentagons forming a net around its surface. Now imagine every intersection on that ball connected radially both inwards and outwards, forming a three-dimensional structure consisting of cellular interconnecting filaments. Here the image of the hexagonal walls of honeycomb inside a beehive are appropriate. The cellular structure inside the spirit sphere is patterned like the beehive, but much less rigidly, certainly not hexagonally, and the filaments extend inwards and outwards throughout the entire globular structure. The interconnecting filaments provide the means by which encoded information is carried through the entire structure.

Encoded within the spiritual identity's globular structure is information regarding what has been done in previous lives and what is intended to be achieved in the new upcoming life. How is information regarding the life plan communicated by the spiritual self to its animal human self? The answer is via the aura. So when a spiritual identity dispatches an aspect of itself into the human realm, the now born and growing human being can access knowledge of all the information encoded in its globular spiritual structure via the aura.

When the body dies and is incinerated or decays, the aura itself dissolves. But in the process of dissolving, all the information contained within the mind of the individual's human physical self is spontaneously uploaded, to use that modern concept, as patterns of information conveyed to the globular spiritual identity through the connecting link of the aura. This is easily achieved, because the identity is bi-located, with its spiritual self and its bodily self nested beside and inside one another. There is no distance for the information to travel. The uploading is direct, spontaneous and instantaneous."

THE MATAPAUA CONVERSATIONS

This book is the first collaboration between Peter and Keith. The circumstances that led to its creation is that after editing Peter's *Guided Healing*, Keith saw an opportunity to exploit Peter's contact with non-embodied identities to question them about the big bang, evolution, the nature of consciousness, and other metaphysical topics. He eventually came up with a list of one hundred "big questions".

Peter took time out at Matapaua Beach to receive the answers. He also kept a diary on the process. The excerpt that follows was spoken to Peter by the guides soon after he arrived at the secluded house where he stayed while channelling the answers to Keith's questions.

"We begin the developmental and systematic aspects of this teaching, fostered and communicated by the man Keith Hill. Given that it is at his request that we respond to his questions, we feel that proper acknowledgement should be made to the facilitative agreement that he has with us and with you. This agreement was made pre-life, of course.

When contemplating engagement with the earthly realm, you both felt there was an opportunity to contribute to a deeper understanding of the human condition. The opportunity was undertaken in a spirit of self-exploration and self-development. It also involved community engagement and company-inspired social development—"company" in this sense is to be interpreted as meaning a social group whose members share a curiosity concerning the dynamics of life and existence.

That said, we may continue in our task. Rereading Capra [Editor: Peter was reading *The Tao of Physics* by Fritjof Capra] is an essential first step for entering an analytical mindset and re-igniting your curiosity regarding the deep domains of description concerning both agapéic space and the realm of reality associated with the questions that you have come here to have answered.

The domain of these questions is extensive. Answering them requires that a boundary-free condition be established within your mind. That is not yet available, so we have set you the task of attending to the explanatory language offered in that text [*The Tao of Physics*] to take your awareness away from the mundane, away from the local, away from the body's senses and preferences, and expanding your awareness towards the foreign, and even the nonsensical. We use that last term in the special sense of being unrelated to the senses.

The mind is, in fact, free to soar into any realm at any moment, for any duration, within any time frame. This means that all of existence is accessible to the unconstrained mind. The frameworks of thought generated by locality, by embodiment, by emotion, by relationship—all these act to constrain the mind and its reach.

That is why self-isolation is required, to bring those unconstrained realms into view. That also gives rise to the need here to have mind-expanding literature at hand to refocus, as you did earlier when observing the night sky, because your perception is then not confined to the atmosphere. And it serves to remind that there are realms upon realms of distance, of phenomena, of locations far away, of unimaginable magnitudes, waiting the tools to make them observable. Those tools (for example, a telescope) are not available here. But the exercise was sufficient to remind him of the extent to which the world is bigger than this room, this body, these emotions, and these thoughts. The universe is correspondingly larger. The realm of all that is is unimaginably larger again. So, through this reminder, we bring that entire realm back into the central awareness as the vista to be explored during our time here."

AGAPÉ AND THE HIERARCHY OF LOVE

Peter's first channelled book uses a wide range of models and metaphors to explore agapé theory. The overall thrust is scientific and secular, reconceiving traditional spiritual concepts in fresh and frequently innovative

116   On Acquiring Wisdom

ways that are consistent with our modern outlook. Topics include the nature of the higher self and its mind and how to establish a connection to it, the thousand life incarnation model, the spiritual nature of love, and an exploration of the implications of agapé theory using models of many different kinds. The following is excerpted from the book's introduction.

"We intend to initiate an international movement towards the study of the impact of the spiritual domain on human life in all its variety, in particular its impact on the theory of being. Where once ground-level knowledge relevant to agriculture for food creation was sufficient, now theory has encompassed the origins and end of the known universe.

The question, then, is what lies beyond that? It was once enough to respond to the heart-felt love emanating from the spiritual domain, which people experienced via visions and in dreams. Now a more dynamic understanding is available that provides direct knowledge of the entities who inhabit the spiritual domain.

Once the current arguments regarding the existence of the spiritual domain are resolved, and a new consensual reality is established that draws on the empirical observations of mystics, a new inclusive outlook will arise. This will make a complete view of reality, that integrates the spiritual and the physical, available to anyone willing to take the time to develop the skills needed to perceive it. Religion in unsophisticated forms will fall away, as simplistic belief will not be required."

GUIDED HEALING

Guided Healing contains two urgent messages. One presents guidance for all spiritual seekers, the other is addressed specifically to potential healers.

To spiritual seekers, *Guided Healing* presents a novel view of the spiritual purpose and benefits of being born into a physical body. Issues covered include the relationship between the spiritual and physical realms, the reason for incarnation, the use of meditation as a means for exploring the spiritual realm, and the significance of soul work.

To healers, *Guided Healing* offers instruction on how to become a conduit for healing energy that emanates from the spiritual realm. Topics covered include how to contact guides in the spiritual realm, the nature of spiritual perception, and factors which enhance or hinder energy flow during the act of healing.

Most significantly, the text introduces the concept of agapéic space as a way to discuss spiritual existence and humanity's role in it. It reveals how agapé – spiritual love – underlies all existence, and what is required of us in order to tune into it.

Using concepts drawn from science and contemporary culture, Guided Healing presents a vision of human spirituality appropriate for our times, as we move out of traditional, paternalistic religious allegories and into a rational appreciation of what being spiritual involves.

PEOPLE OF THE EARTH

"I have always considered the nature of our embodiment the most important unresolved issue of our civilisation. Peter Calvert and his colleagues have made an ambitious attempt to communicate with disembodied life forms. The fact that these dialogues are of varying clarity, alien credibility, and internal continuity is not as important as the acts of faith that generated them. The urgent truth is that we have to begin somewhere if we are going to explore tabooed portals, claim our place in the greater universe, and find the wisdom necessary to redeem our own world."

— Richard Grossinger, author of *The Night Sky: Soul and Cosmos* and *Bottoming Out the Universe: Why Is There Something Rather Than Nothing?*

People of the Earth offers a unique account of communications with spiritual identities normally invisible to us: deceased people lost between worlds, nature spirits who nurture the Earth's ecosystems, and non-human beings who "drop in" to see what is going on. It challenges our assumptions regarding life and death, and asks us to reconsider who else may be sharing the universe with us.

When Peter Calvert gathered a small group of meditators and set them the task of opening their minds to whoever arrived, he didn't anticipate the astonishing encounters that would result. They discovered a small percentage of people become confused after death. Lost in a transitional zone, they need guidance to move on to the next phase of their existence.

And in a series of vexed visits, nature spirits pleaded with the meditators to share an urgent message with humanity regarding the dire state of the planet's ecosystems.

Through a sequence of intriguing dialogues between the meditators and visiting non-embodied beings, *People of the Earth* provides sobering insights to those who seek to understand what is required of us spiritually to sustain the planet's ecological health.

THE CHANNELLED SPIRITUALITY SERIES

The Channelled Spirituality Series provides for those who wish to engage in their own personal development. It provides a means for seekers to understand their individual psychospiritual make-up, what factors drive their current existence, and what the key factors of their life plan involve. In this sense, *The Channelled Spirituality Series* offers a practical way to carry out self-enquiry. Channelled by Keith Hill.

EXPERIMENTAL SPIRITUALITY

This first book in the series introduces the rationale for adopting a non-religious, empirical and experimental approach to spirituality. Topics covered include how to treat beliefs as propositions and not as truths, how spirituality involves a journey from belief to understanding, and how finding answers depends on asking the right questions. The book also introduces the model of the five-layered self as an aid to understanding the human psyche.

"By now it will be clear to readers the extent to which beliefs of all kinds are naturally generated by the human everyday awareness during its daily interactions. Many beliefs are totally innocuous, such as the belief that an apple a day will keep the doctor away. Other beliefs involve practical necessities, such as the belief a light will turn on when you flick the switch. And some beliefs reflect truths about the world, such as the belief that the Earth travels around the Sun. In this last case such belief is better described as knowledge.

As was stated earlier, a particular belief is no more than an assumption until it has been tested and the tester has ascertained whether or not it reflects reality. Tested and validated beliefs become the basis of new knowledge. Because individuals have different experiences, and because people often draw quite different conclusions from the same experiences, there is an extensive range of positions from belief to knowledge. And even within this range there are those at the extremities, such as those who espouse lunatic beliefs and those who express extensively tested knowledge. This latter category applies both to knowledge obtained through objective scientific testing and to knowledge garnered as a result of interrogating one's own assumptions and outlook and tempering them in the fires of personal experience.

It is, of course, mere common sense to draw attention to this range from the lunatic to the knowing. Anyone who gives the idea a moment of attention can easily verify it from their own experience, and can further verify how the very different functioning of people's everyday awareness accounts for the huge differences between assumed beliefs and hard won knowledge. Accordingly, from the spiritual perspective advocated here, the principal point that needs to be made is that beliefs are held by immature individuals or cultures, whereas knowledge is in the possession of the mature.

When two people argue over their belief or non-belief in God they are each indulging in childish behaviour—because they are arguing over beliefs, not knowledge. Of course, each side maintains what they believe with great intensity. Each considers they know The Truth and that those they oppose do not. But thinking you know is not the same as actually knowing. Neither is holding intensely to a belief the same as actually knowing.

Until a belief has been rigorously tested it is nothing more than an assumption. And an assumption should be considered as only a starting point on the journey towards knowledge. This is the journey from immaturity to maturity."

PRACTICAL SPIRITUALITY

The second book begins a consideration of the psychological factors that we draw in when selecting our next incarnation, along with all the other factors that are involved. Topics include: the characteristics of core disposition that makes each human being a unique spiritual identity; what is involved in selecting a life plan; seeking our bliss; the creation and resolution of karmic relationships; life lessons; and mastering the art of incarnation.

This book also extensively adds to the model of the five-layered self introduced in *Experimental Spirituality*, showing how it is an effective tool for seekers to understand their complex psyche. The following is an excerpt that discusses the contribution one's life goal makes to the life plan.

"Psychologically, every human being has a single defining essence level life goal. This life goal denotes a fundamental approach to living that the spiritual identity has adopted. It underpins everything the individual is striving to achieve during this life.

The individual draws on a number of factors when deciding how it will live its next incarnation. These include positive and negative deep essence qualities developed during previous lives, essence traits innate to the next body's genetic disposition, karma that is to be worked through, and agreements to meet certain other incarnated people to help achieve mutually agreed tasks. All these are part of an individual's life plan.

Another key contributor to the life plan is the individual's life goal. The life goal is a psychological characteristic that functions at the essence level. There are seven in total. We note that the life goal is not the same as what is generally referred to as life goals.

Life goals are specific pragmatic physical and social goals individuals set themselves to achieve during the course of a week, a month, a year, or even a lifetime. Life goals include taking part in a competition, establishing a career, having a family, becoming wealthy, dedicating one's life to helping the underprivileged, becoming a country's president or prime minister, or not being like one's parents or siblings. Life goals may be large or small. But they are physically or socially defined, and they all involve a series of steps or tasks that need to be accomplished in order to ensure the chosen life goals is achieved. We call these life tasks.

In contrast, the *life goal* doesn't involve a particular task or series of tasks. The life goal may be thought of as psychological glue that underpins all the various aims, tasks, agreements, karmic debts, and essence activities that the individual chooses to carry out during the course of a life. As such, the life goal is aligned to each individual's life plan. The life goal defines the individual's overall approach to a life. Drawing on the Michael Teachings, we identify seven fundamental types of life goal. These seven are: growth, revaluation, dominance, submission, acceptance, rejection and maintaining equilibrium.

Each of these identifies what, in global terms, an individual seeks to achieve in a particular life. It identifies an individual's approach, that is, an individual's essence level psychological predisposition, when faced with choices and alternative possibilities during any life."

PSYCHOLOGICAL SPIRITUALITY

This book is paired with *Practical Spirituality*, as the guides required two books to fully explore the impact of reincarnation on human psychology. The concept of accumulated human identity is introduced to account for what is uploaded from a life to the spiritual self, then used in a later life. Other key concepts include: the role of fear in shaping childhood behavioural coping mechanisms that extend into adulthood; how fear lays the foundations for chief feature, the conflict between true and false personality; how the nature of life plans progressively change through our entire cycle of incarnations; how to change our psychological momentum; the need to think of ourselves as multi-life identities; and the key factors of orientation and attitude.

"To begin this discussion of how false personality stops you from fully achieving your life plan, let's summarise your life situation. You are born into a body that has certain genetic predispositions. The family and social environment in which you are raised imposes specific attitudes, beliefs and behaviours on you. Because human existence is complex and difficult, you develop defensive behaviours to help you cope with trying situations. These self-defensive behaviours are gathered around a chief feature that has a specific fear at its core. Over time these fear-based self-defensive traits become imbedded in your socialised self.

You also have an essence self. Your essence self is an expression of your spiritual self. It is the higher human part of you that is seeking to fulfil specific tasks, develop skills, foster abilities, and express talents. It is the best of your human sub-personality this time round. But in order for you to work with other people, your essence self has to express itself via your socialised self.

Your socialised self possesses a number of neutral traits that enable you to interact effectively with others: language, customs, socially agreed ways of behaving. But it also has a dark side, consisting of your deep fears, your chief feature, and buried defensive attitudes. Collectively, these dark aspects of your socialised self are inhibitory mechanisms that hinder your essence self's efforts. We are calling these fear-centered, self-defensive, inhibitory traits false personality. Psychologically, they have their own momentum within you, their own inertial mass. And this momentum leaks into and impacts on your essence self.

As a result no one's life momentum is optimal. No one is implementing every single aspect of their life plan to its maximum potential. We don't say this to deflate you. Far from it. We say it because the fact is that no one lives their life without at least some negative impact from false personality. Everyone has experienced times when fear, or lack of confidence, or over-confidence, or second-guesssing, or defensiveness, or any of many other traits, caused them to hesitate and not do what deep down they wanted to do. This is how false personality causes you to depart from your life plan—not by offering you an equally compelling new goal, but by stopping you making progress at all."

www.ingramcontent.com/pod-product-compliance
Lightning Source LLC
Chambersburg PA
CBHW020427010526
44118CB00010B/456